"Crafting Your Perfect Picnic Table"

This book delves into the creation of a specific and highly sought-after style of picnic table. There are eight detailed project plans, each showcasing the same picnic table design in various dimensions.

While the style and construction method remain consistent across all projects, the sizes vary. By following the project plans provided, you'll be equipped to build a traditional picnic table ranging from 6½ feet (2 meters) up to an impressive 12 feet (3.6 meters) - pick a size to suit.

Additionally, you'll have the flexibility to choose between two common lumber sizes: 2 x 6 (50 x 150 mm) or 2 x 4 (50 x 100 mm).

So, not only will you take pride in constructing your own picnic table, but you'll also relish its use for years to come.

The designs in this book showcase sturdy, solid picnic tables featuring wider tabletops compared to most standard designs

Build Your Own Picnic Table

Color version

A card by card - Step by step guide.
The same great design in various sizes.

A selection of picnic tables to make - from 6½ feet (2 meters) up to 12 feet (3.6 meters) in size.
Simply follow the cards

By Les Kenny

Les Kenny, 1948-.

Build Your Own Picnic Table

Color version

Copyright © Les Kenny 2024

All rights reserved.

Les Kenny asserts the moral right to be identified as the author of this work.

ISBN 978-1-7635730-0-0

leskenny.com

CONTENTS

Jump to a project - *Just follow the cards*

Six seater picnic table Using 2 x 4 (50 x 100 mm) lumber	Card 01
Six seater picnic table Using 2 x 6 (50 x 150 mm) lumber	Card 33
Eight seater picnic table Using 2 x 4 (50 x 100 mm) lumber	Card 65
Eight seater picnic table Using 2 x 6 (50 x 150 mm) lumber	Card 97
Ten seater picnic table Using 2 x 4 (50 x 100 mm) lumber	Card 129
Ten seater picnic table Using 2 x 6 (50 x 150 mm) lumber	Card 161
Twelve seater picnic table Using 2 x 4 (50 x 100 mm) lumber	Card 193
Twelve seater picnic table Using 2 x 6 (50 x 150 mm) lumber	Card 225
Information Cards	Card 257

Build your own Picnic Table

6-1/2 feet (2 meter) long

Using 2 x 4 (50 x 100 mm) lumber

It will comfortably seat 6 people

Just follow the cards →

Card 01

Build Your Own Picnic Table

* 6½ feet (2 meters) long
* Using 2 x 4 (50 x 100 mm) lumber

Just follow the cards

Card 02

Picnic Table Project
• 6½ feet (2 meters) long
• Using 2 x 4 (50 x 100 mm) lumber

Description

This picnic table is constructed out of 2 x 4 (50 x 100 mm) lumber. It will comfortably seat 6 people. Wide seats positioned both in terms of height and distance from the tabletop ensures easy access and maximum comfort.

Dimensions:
- Length: 6' 6¾" (2 m).
- Width: 67" (1700 mm).
- Height: 29⅞" (758 mm).
- Tabletop width: 34¼" (870 mm).

Card 03

Picnic Table Project
• 6½ feet (2 meters) long
• Using 2 x 4 (50 x 100 mm) lumber

Table of Contents - 1

Description	Card 02
Part identification	Card 05
Plans: Imperial measurements	Card 06
Plans: Metric measurements	Card 07
About the measurements	Card 08
Shopping list: Lumber	Card 09
Shopping list: Fixings	Card 10
Cutting list	Card 12
Cut the components to length	Card 14
Cutting plan	Card 15

Card 04

Picnic Table Project
• 6½ feet (2 meters) long
• Using 2 x 4 (50 x 100 mm) lumber

Table of Contents - 2

Cut the angled pieces	Card 16
Arrange the legs	Card 18
Assemble the end frames	Card 19
Stand the frames	Card 21
Put on the outer boards	Card 23
Check for square and parallel	Card 25
Add the intermediate boards	Card 27
Attach the cleats	Card 29
Add bracing	Card 30
Drill and bolt	Card 31

Picnic Table Project
Card 05
- 6½ feet (2 meters) long
- Using 2 x 4 (50 x 100 mm) lumber

Part identification

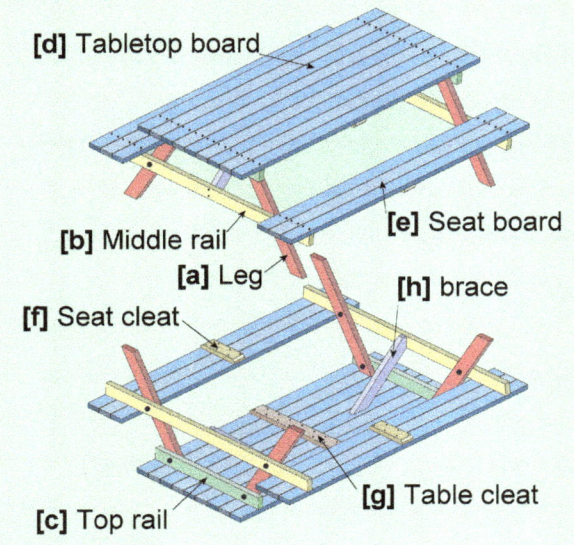

- [d] Tabletop board
- [b] Middle rail
- [a] Leg
- [e] Seat board
- [h] brace
- [f] Seat cleat
- [g] Table cleat
- [c] Top rail

Picnic Table Project
Card 06
- 6½ feet (2 meters) long
- Using 2 x 4 (50 x 100 mm) lumber

Plans: Imperial measurements

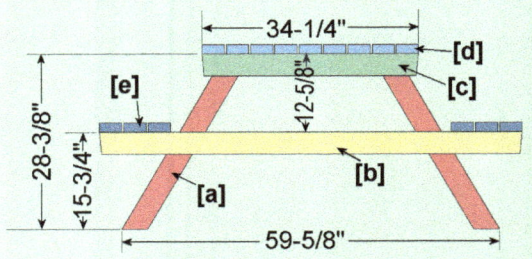

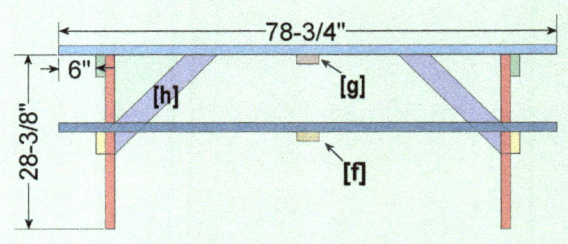

Picnic Table Project
Card 07
- 6½ feet (2 meters) long
- Using 2 x 4 (50 x 100 mm) lumber

Plans: Metric measurements

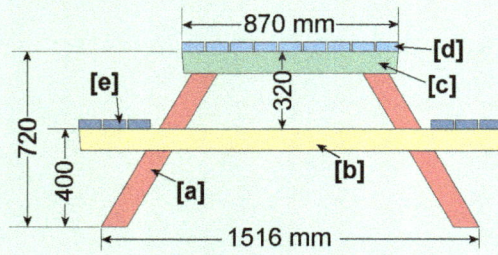

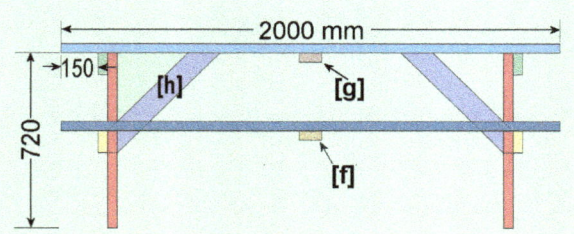

Picnic Table Project
Card 08
- 6½ feet (2 meters) long
- Using 2 x 4 (50 x 100 mm) lumber

About the measurements

Length measurements in this project are given in both imperial units (inches) and metric units (millimeters).

When the measurements are presented side by side, the inch measurements are given first followed by the metric equivalent in brackets.

For example: 15-3/4" (400 mm).

Card 09

Picnic Table Project
- 6½ feet (2 meters) long
- Using 2 x 4 (50 x 100 mm) lumber

Shopping list: Lumber

Wood size	Length	Qty
2 x 4 (50 x 100 mm)	8 ft (2.4 m)	10
2 x 4 (50 x 100 mm)	10 ft (3 m)	7

The lengths provided above are standard stock sizes.
From those lengths you will be able to cut all the pieces that are required to construct the picnic table.
Card 15 shows how you can cut all the pieces from the above lengths to minimize waste.

Card 10

Picnic Table Project
- 6½ feet (2 meters) long
- Using 2 x 4 (50 x 100 mm) lumber

Shopping list: Fixings

Exterior wood screws:
- 72 screws 3" (75 mm) long.
- 60 screws 3½" (90 mm) long.

1/2" (12 mm) galvanized coach/carriage bolts:
- 8 bolts 4" (100 mm) long.
- 8 each nuts and washers to match.

Note: Use the 3" (75 mm) screws for the frames, cleats, and braces.
Use the 3½" (90 mm) screws for the seat boards and the tabletop boards.

Card 11

Picnic Table Project
- 6½ feet (2 meters) long
- Using 2 x 4 (50 x 100 mm) lumber

Dressed lumber

Dressed lumber is wood that has been planed and smoothed, which makes it smaller than the nominal sizes given.

For example, 2 x 4 (50 x 100 mm) dressed lumber will be 1½" x 3½" (38 x 89 mm) in actual size.

Note: The difference in size will not impact the build, as it is the lengths of the pieces that are important, not so much the size (width and thickness) of the wood.

Card 12

Picnic Table Project
- 6½ feet (2 meters) long
- Using 2 x 4 (50 x 100 mm) lumber

Cutting list

2 x 4 (50 x 100 mm) lumber		
Piece ID	Length	Qty
[a]	34¾" (883 mm)	4
[b]	67" (1700 mm)	2
[c]	34¼" (870 mm)	2
[d]	78¾" (2000 mm)	9
[e]	78¾" (2000 mm)	6
[f]	11¼" (285 mm)	2
[g]	34¼" (870 mm)	1
[h]	25" (635 mm)	2

Picnic Table Project
- 6½ feet (2 meters) long
- Using 2 x 4 (50 x 100 mm) lumber

Card 13

INSTRUCTIONS

Let's Go!

Start the build

Just follow the cards

Picnic Table Project
- 6½ feet (2 meters) long
- Using 2 x 4 (50 x 100 mm) lumber

Card 14

Cut all the pieces

All lumber is 2 x 4 (50 x 100 mm) stock.

Cut all the pieces to the lengths given in the 'Cutting list' (**Card 12**).

All the pieces can be cut from the standard stock lengths that are listed in the 'Shopping list' (**Card 09**).

Following on the next card is a plan drawing showing how all the pieces can be cut from the standard lengths of lumber given in the 'Shopping list'.

Picnic Table Project
- 6½ feet (2 meters) long
- Using 2 x 4 (50 x 100 mm) lumber

Card 15

Cutting plan

The drawing below demonstrates how to cut all the components from the following pieces of 2 x 4 (50 x 100 mm) lumber.
- 10 pieces 8 ft (2.4 m) long.
- 7 pieces 10 ft (3 m) long.

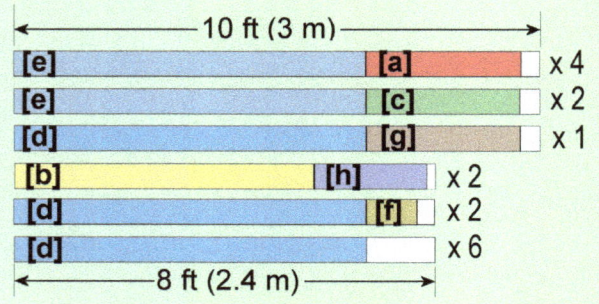

Picnic Table Project
- 6½ feet (2 meters) long
- Using 2 x 4 (50 x 100 mm) lumber

Card 16

Cut the angled pieces

Once all the pieces are cut to length, pieces **[a]**, **[b]**, **[c]**, and **[h]** need to have the ends cut at an angle. Cut the angles according to the drawings below.

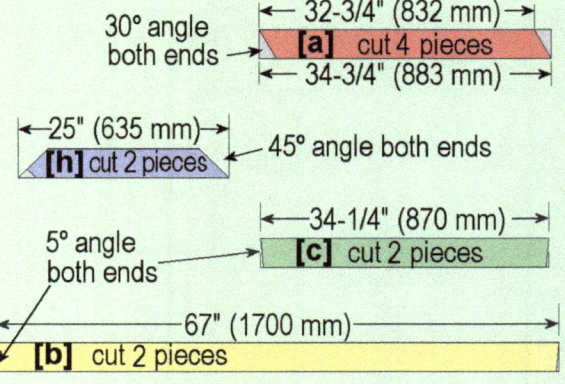

Picnic Table Project
- 6½ feet (2 meters) long
- Using 2 x 4 (50 x 100 mm) lumber

Card 17

Ready to assemble

At this stage, you should have all the pieces cut as shown below, ready for assembly.

- [a] Leg — 4 pieces
- [b] Middle rail — 2 pieces
- [c] Top rail — 2 pieces
- [d] Tabletop board — 9 pieces
- [e] Seat board — 6 pieces
- [f] Seat cleat — 2 pieces
- [g] Table cleat — 1 piece
- [h] Brace — 2 pieces

Picnic Table Project
- 6½ feet (2 meters) long
- Using 2 x 4 (50 x 100 mm) lumber

Card 18

Arrange the legs

Lay each pair of legs flat on an even surface, spaced according to the plan drawing below. Use a straight-edge to ensure the bottom of both legs are in-line.

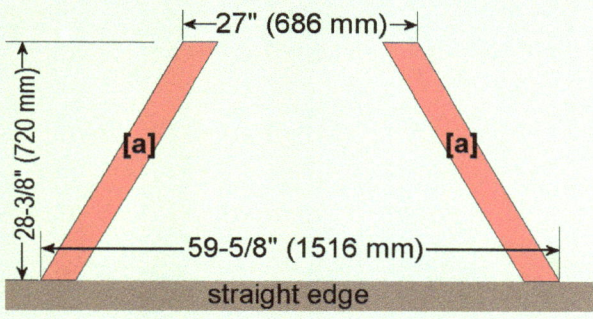

Picnic Table Project
- 6½ feet (2 meters) long
- Using 2 x 4 (50 x 100 mm) lumber

Card 19

Assemble the end frames

Place cross rails [b] and [c] on legs [a] according to the plan drawing below. Use four 3" (75 mm) screws at each joint, as illustrated in the drawing. Do not place screws in the middle of a joint, as that space is reserved for a bolt.

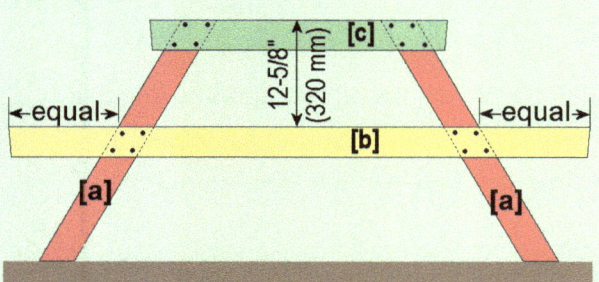

Picnic Table Project
- 6½ feet (2 meters) long
- Using 2 x 4 (50 x 100 mm) lumber

Card 20

Screwing

Whenever you're fastening two pieces of wood together with screws, it's important to predrill a **clearance hole** through the top piece.

A **clearance hole** should have the same diameter or slightly larger (but never smaller) than the outside diameter of the screw threads.

This allows the screw to go through the top piece smoothly, with the threads only gripping into the bottom piece, ensuring a tight connection between the two parts.

Picnic Table Project
- 6½ feet (2 meters) long
- Using 2 x 4 (50 x 100 mm) lumber

Card 21

Stand the end frames

Clamp a block flush to the bottom of each leg, as illustrated in the drawing below. This allows the frames to stand by themselves. Hence, you can position the frames and place the boards without needing help from another person to hold the frames upright.

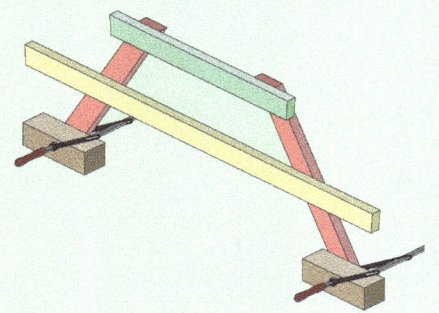

Picnic Table Project
- 6½ feet (2 meters) long
- Using 2 x 4 (50 x 100 mm) lumber

Card 22

Arrange the end frames

Now, space the frames approximately so that when the tabletop and seat boards are positioned, they will overhang the frames at each end by 6" (150 mm).

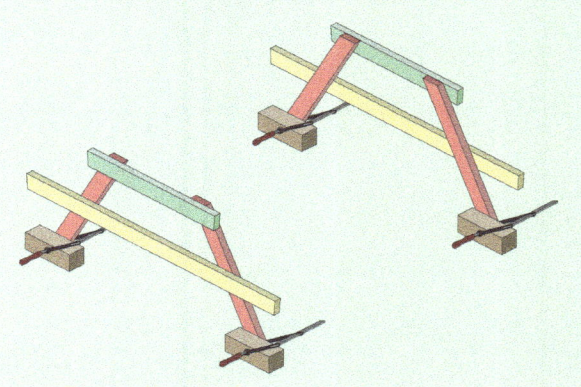

Picnic Table Project
- 6½ feet (2 meters) long
- Using 2 x 4 (50 x 100 mm) lumber

Card 23

Put on the outer boards

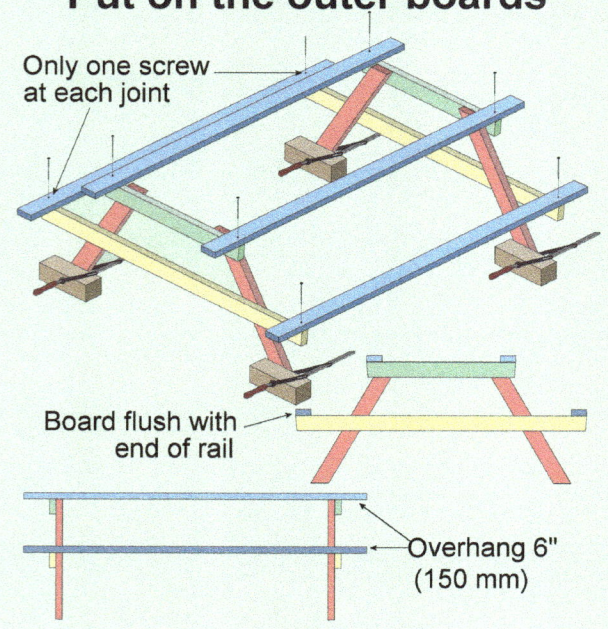

Only one screw at each joint

Board flush with end of rail

Overhang 6" (150 mm)

Picnic Table Project
- 6½ feet (2 meters) long
- Using 2 x 4 (50 x 100 mm) lumber

Card 24

Put on the outer boards [explanation]

First, place the outer tabletop and seat boards onto the frame rails, having them overhang each end by 6" (150 mm). Refer to the drawing on the previous card for placement

Secure the boards with <u>**only one screw**</u> at each joint - for the time being.

A second screw will be added when the frames have been checked square and parallel. Use 3½" (90 mm) screws positioned ⅝" (15 mm) in from the edge of the board.

Picnic Table Project
- 6½ feet (2 meters) long
- Using 2 x 4 (50 x 100 mm) lumber

Card 25

Is it square and parallel?

Carpenters square horizontal check

LOOKING DOWN VIEW

Carpenters square vertical check

SIDE VIEW

Picnic Table Project
- 6½ feet (2 meters) long
- Using 2 x 4 (50 x 100 mm) lumber

Card 26

Is it square and parallel? [explanation]

Check that the frames are parallel, and with a carpenter's square ensure the frames are square (at right angles) to the tabletop and seat boards, both horizontally and vertically. If necessary, make any straightening adjustments, then add a second screw to each joint.

This will hold the unit square while you continue to add the intermediate boards.

Picnic Table Project
- 6½ feet (2 meters) long
- Using 2 x 4 (50 x 100 mm) lumber

Card 27

Add the intermediate boards

Place the intermediate boards. Ensure the ends are flush and the gaps between the boards are even.

Draw a 'screw line' across the table and seats to keep the screws in a straight line.

Picnic Table Project
- 6½ feet (2 meters) long
- Using 2 x 4 (50 x 100 mm) lumber

Card 28

Screwing detail

Use 3½" (90 mm) exterior wood screws. Ensure the screws are in a straight line purely for aesthetic purposes.

Drill clearance holes through the top boards prior to screwing.

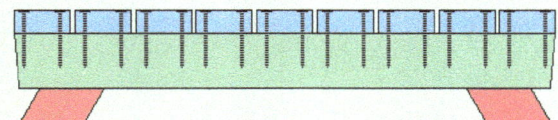

Picnic Table Project
Card 29
- *6½ feet (2 meters) long*
- *Using 2 x 4 (50 x 100 mm) lumber*

Attach the cleats

With the table upside-down, screw cleats across the center of the seats and the tabletop. Use two 3" (75 mm) screws positioned diagonally across each joint.

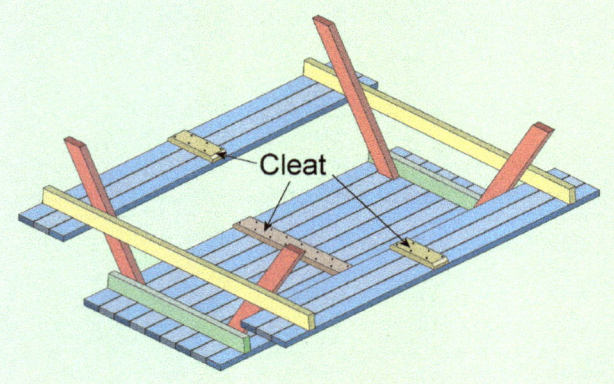

Picnic Table Project
Card 30
- *6½ feet (2 meters) long*
- *Using 2 x 4 (50 x 100 mm) lumber*

Add bracing

Ensure the end-frames are square (upright) to the tabletop, and then position each brace as shown in the image below. Screw one end of the brace to the middle rail with two 3" (75 mm) screws, and the other end with 3 screws angled into the tabletop.

Picnic Table Project
Card 31
- *6½ feet (2 meters) long*
- *Using 2 x 4 (50 x 100 mm) lumber*

Drill and bolt

Drill a bolt hole through the center of every leg and rail joint - eight altogether.
Insert 1/2" (12 mm) galvanised bolts, add washers and nuts, and tighten them up.

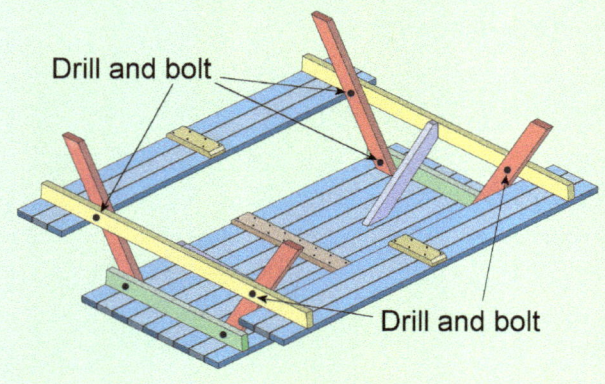

Picnic Table Project
Card 32
- *6½ feet (2 meters) long*
- *Using 2 x 4 (50 x 100 mm) lumber*

All finished!

And there it is.
A nice solid, comfortable picnic table that will seat at least six people.

Enjoy!

You are now leaving the
6-1/2 feet (2 meters) long picnic table project
constructed out of
2 x 4 (50 x 100 mm) lumber

Next up
6-1/2 feet (2 meters) long picnic table project
using
2 x 6 (50 x 150 mm) lumber

Build your own Picnic Table

6-1/2 feet (2 meters) long

Using 2 x 6 (50 x 150 mm) lumber

It will comfortably seat 6 people

Just follow the cards →

Card 33

Build Your Own Picnic Table

* *6½ feet (2 meters) long*
* *Using 2 x 6 (50 x 150 mm) lumber*

Just follow the cards

Card 34

Picnic Table Project
• *6½ feet (2 meters) long*
• *Using 2 x 6 (50 x 150 mm) lumber*

Description

This picnic table is constructed out of 2 x 6 (50 x 150 mm) lumber. It will comfortably seat 6 people. Wide seats positioned both in terms of height and distance from the tabletop ensures easy access and maximum comfort.

Dimensions:
- Length: 6' 6¾" (2 meters).
- Width: 67" (1700 mm).
- Height: 29⅞" (758 mm).
- Tabletop width: 34¼" (870 mm).

Card 35

Picnic Table Project
• *6½ feet (2 meters) long*
• *Using 2 x 6 (50 x 150 mm) lumber*

Table of Contents - 1

Description	Card 34
Part identification	Card 37
Plans: Imperial measurements	Card 38
Plans: Metric measurements	Card 39
About the measurements	Card 40
Shopping list: Lumber	Card 41
Shopping list: Fixings	Card 42
Cutting list	Card 44
Cut the components to length	Card 46
Cutting plan	Card 47

Card 36

Picnic Table Project
• *6½ feet (2 meters) long*
• *Using 2 x 6 (50 x 150 mm) lumber*

Table of Contents - 2

Cut the angled pieces	Card 48
Arrange the legs	Card 50
Assemble the end frames	Card 51
Stand the frames	Card 53
Put on the outer boards	Card 55
Check for square and parallel	Card 57
Add the intermediate boards	Card 59
Attach the cleats	Card 61
Add bracing	Card 62
Drill and bolt	Card 63

Picnic Table Project
Card 37
- 6½ feet (2 meters) long
- Using 2 x 6 (50 x 150 mm) lumber

Part identification

[d] Tabletop board
[c] Top rail
[g] Table cleat
[f] Seat cleat
[h] Brace
[e] Seat board
[a] Leg
[b] Middle rail

Picnic Table Project
Card 38
- 6½ feet (2 meters) long
- Using 2 x 6 (50 x 150 mm) lumber

Plans - Imperial units

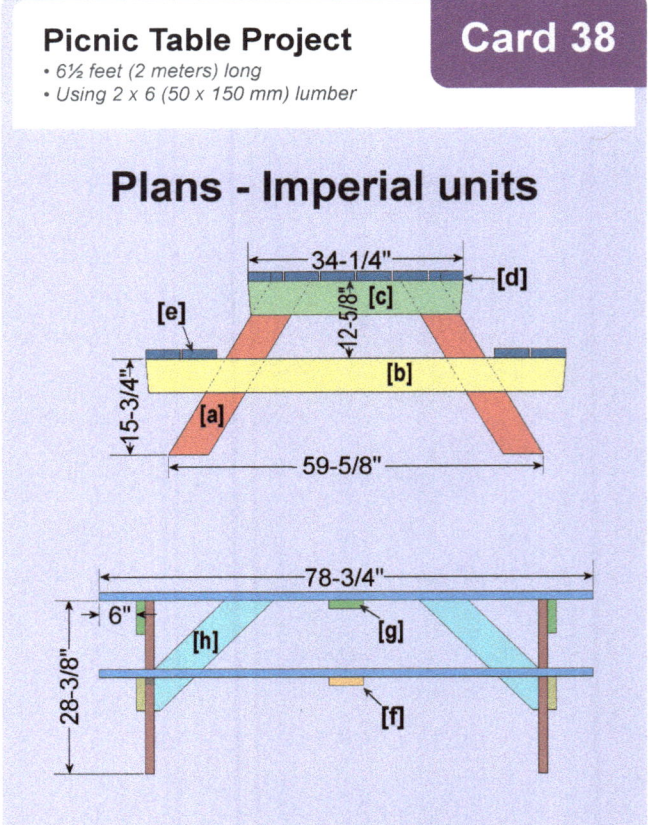

Picnic Table Project
Card 39
- 6½ feet (2 meters) long
- Using 2 x 6 (50 x 150 mm) lumber

Plans - Metric units

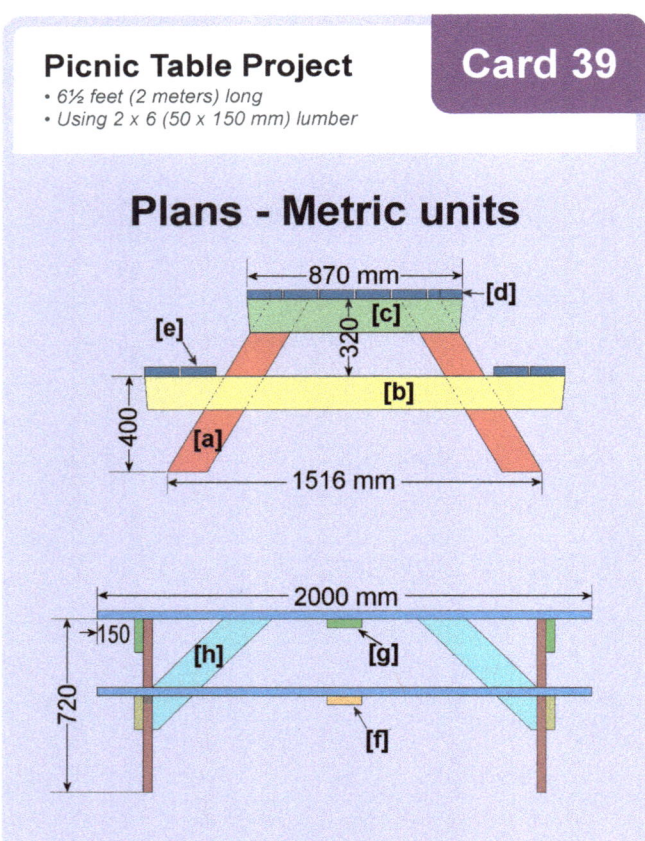

Picnic Table Project
Card 40
- 6½ feet (2 meters) long
- Using 2 x 6 (50 x 150 mm) lumber

About the measurements

Length measurements in this project are given in both imperial units (inches) and metric units (millimeters).

When the measurements are presented side by side, the inch measurements are given first followed by the metric equivalent in brackets.

For example: 15-3/4" (400 mm).

Picnic Table Project
- 6½ feet (2 meters) long
- Using 2 x 6 (50 x 150 mm) lumber

Card 41

Shopping list: Lumber

Wood size	Length	Qty
2 x 6 (50 x 150 mm)	8 ft (2.4 m)	2
2 x 6 (50 x 150 mm)	10 ft (3 m)	7
2 x 6 (50 x 150 mm)	12 ft (3.6 m)	2

From the lengths provided above you will be able to cut all the pieces that are required to construct the picnic table.

Card 47 shows how you can cut all the pieces from the above lengths to minimize waste.

Picnic Table Project
- 6½ feet (2 meters) long
- Using 2 x 6 (50 x 150 mm) lumber

Card 42

Shopping list: Fixings

Exterior wood screws:
- 62 screws 3" (75 mm) long.
- 40 screws 3½" (90 mm) long.

1/2" (12 mm) galvanized coach/carriage bolts:
- 8 bolts 4" (100 mm) long.
- 8 each nuts and washers to match.

Note: Use the 3" (75 mm) screws for the frames, cleats, and braces.
Use the 3½" (90 mm) screws for the seat boards and the tabletop boards.

Picnic Table Project
- 6½ feet (2 meters) long
- Using 2 x 6 (50 x 150 mm) lumber

Card 43

Dressed lumber

Dressed lumber is wood that has been planed and smoothed, which makes it smaller than the nominal sizes given.

For example, 2 x 6 (50 x 150 mm) dressed lumber will be 1½" x 5½" (38 x 140 mm) in actual size.

Note: The difference in size will not impact the build, as it is the lengths of the pieces that are important, not so much the size (width and thickness) of the wood.

Picnic Table Project
- 6½ feet (2 meters) long
- Using 2 x 6 (50 x 150 mm) lumber

Card 44

Cutting list

2 x 6 (50 x 150 mm) lumber		
Piece ID	Length	Qty
[a]	36" (912 mm)	4
[b]	67" (1700 mm)	2
[c]	34¼" (870 mm)	2
[d]	78¾" (2000 mm)	6
[e]	78¾" (2000 mm)	4
[f]	11¼" (285 mm)	2
[g]	34¼" (870 mm)	1
[h]	28⅞" (734 mm)	2

Picnic Table Project
- 6½ feet (2 meters) long
- Using 2 x 6 (50 x 150 mm) lumber

Card 45

INSTRUCTIONS

Let's Go!

Start the build

Just follow the cards

Picnic Table Project
- 6½ feet (2 meters) long
- Using 2 x 6 (50 x 150 mm) lumber

Card 46

Cut all the pieces

All lumber is 2 x 6 (50 x 150 mm) stock.

Cut all the pieces to the lengths given in the 'Cutting list' (**Card 44**).

All the pieces can be cut from the standard stock lengths that are listed in the 'Shopping list' (**Card 41**).

Following on the next card is a plan drawing showing how all the pieces can be cut from the standard lengths of lumber given in the 'Shopping list'.

Picnic Table Project
- 6½ feet (2 meters) long
- Using 2 x 6 (50 x 150 mm) lumber

Card 47

Cutting plan

Using 2 x 6 (50 x 150 mm) lumber, You can extract (cut) all the pieces from the following stock lengths

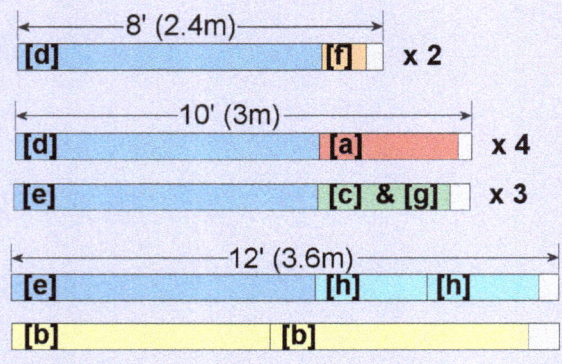

Picnic Table Project
- 6½ feet (2 meters) long
- Using 2 x 6 (50 x 150 mm) lumber

Card 48

Cut the angles pieces

Once all the pieces are cut to length, pieces **[a]**, **[b]**, **[c]**, and **[h]** need to have the ends cut at an angle. Cut the angles according to the drawings below.

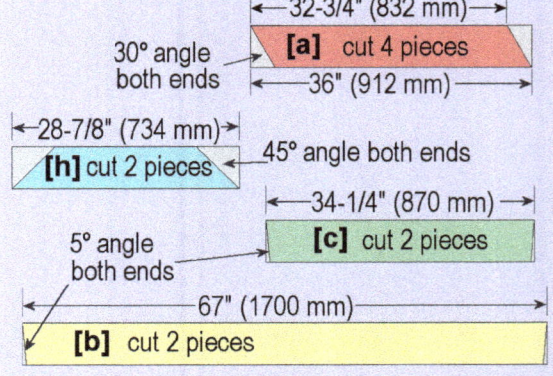

Picnic Table Project
- 6½ feet (2 meters) long
- Using 2 x 6 (50 x 150 mm) lumber

Card 49

Ready to assemble

At this stage, you should have all the pieces cut as shown below, ready for assembly.

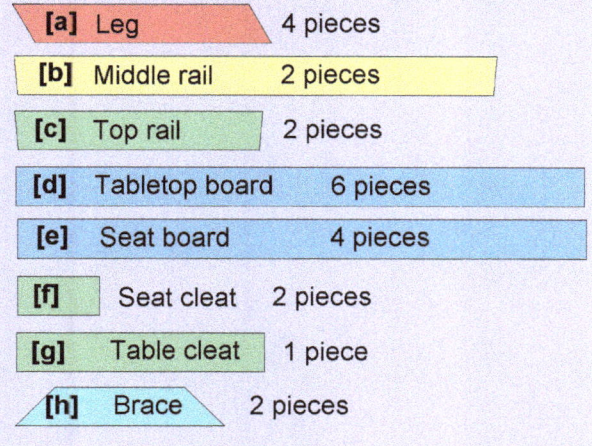

- [a] Leg — 4 pieces
- [b] Middle rail — 2 pieces
- [c] Top rail — 2 pieces
- [d] Tabletop board — 6 pieces
- [e] Seat board — 4 pieces
- [f] Seat cleat — 2 pieces
- [g] Table cleat — 1 piece
- [h] Brace — 2 pieces

Picnic Table Project
- 6½ feet (2 meters) long
- Using 2 x 6 (50 x 150 mm) lumber

Card 50

Arrange the legs

Lay each pair of legs flat on an even surface, spacing them according to the plan drawing below. Use a straightedge to ensure the bottom of both legs are in-line.

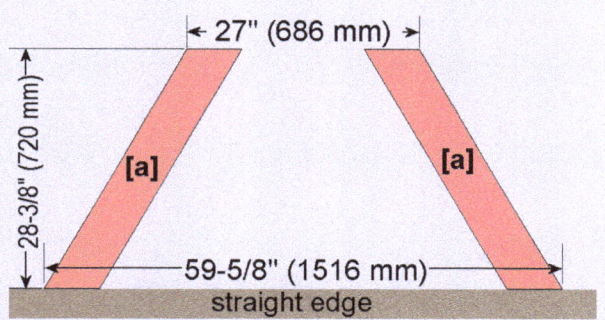

Picnic Table Project
- 6½ feet (2 meters) long
- Using 2 x 6 (50 x 150 mm) lumber

Card 51

Assemble the end frames

Place cross rails [b] and [c] on legs [a] according to the plan drawing below.
Use four 3" (75 mm) screws at each joint, as illustrated in the drawing below. Do not place screws in the middle of a joint, as that space is reserved for a bolt.

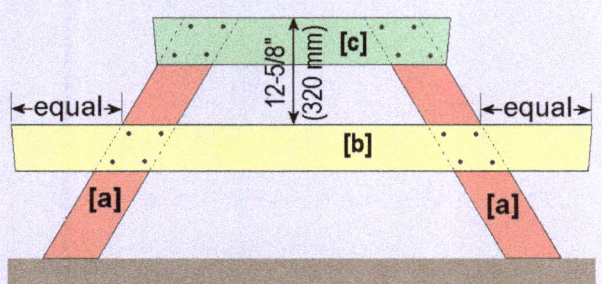

Picnic Table Project
- 6½ feet (2 meters) long
- Using 2 x 6 (50 x 150 mm) lumber

Card 52

 # Screwing

Whenever you're fastening two pieces of wood together with screws, it's important to predrill a **clearance hole** through the top piece.

A **clearance hole** should have the same diameter or slightly larger (but never smaller) than the outside diameter of the screw threads.
This allows the screw to go through the top piece smoothly, with the threads only gripping into the bottom piece, ensuring a tight connection between the two parts.

Picnic Table Project
- 6½ feet (2 meters) long
- Using 2 x 6 (50 x 150 mm) lumber

Card 53

Stand the end frames

Clamp a block flush to the bottom of each leg, as illustrated in the drawing below. This will allow the frames to stand by themselves. Hence, you can position the frames and place the boards without needing help from another person to hold the frames upright.

Picnic Table Project
- 6½ feet (2 meters) long
- Using 2 x 6 (50 x 150 mm) lumber

Card 54

Arrange the end frames

Now, space the frames approximately so that when the tabletop and seat boards are positioned, they will overhang the frames at each end by 6 inches (150 mm).

Picnic Table Project
- 6½ feet (2 meters) long
- Using 2 x 6 (50 x 150 mm) lumber

Card 55

Put on the outer boards

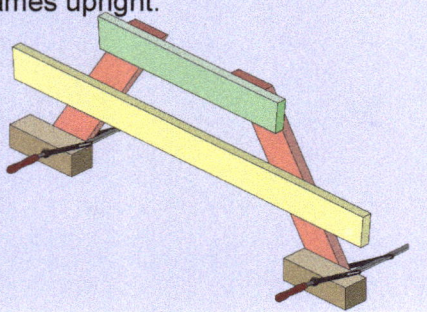

Only one screw at each joint

Board flush with end of rail

Overhang 6" (150 mm)

Picnic Table Project
- 6½ feet (2 meters) long
- Using 2 x 6 (50 x 150 mm) lumber

Card 56

Put on the outer boards [explanation]

First, place the outer tabletop and seat boards onto the frame rails, having them overhang each end by 6" (150 mm). Refer to the drawing on the previous card for placement.

Secure the boards with **only one screw** at each joint - for the time being. A second screw will be added when the frames have been checked square and parallel.

Use 3½" (90 mm) screws and position them in ¾" (19 mm) from the edge of the board.

Picnic Table Project
Card 57
- 6½ feet (2 meters) long
- Using 2 x 6 (50 x 150 mm) lumber

Is it square and parallel?

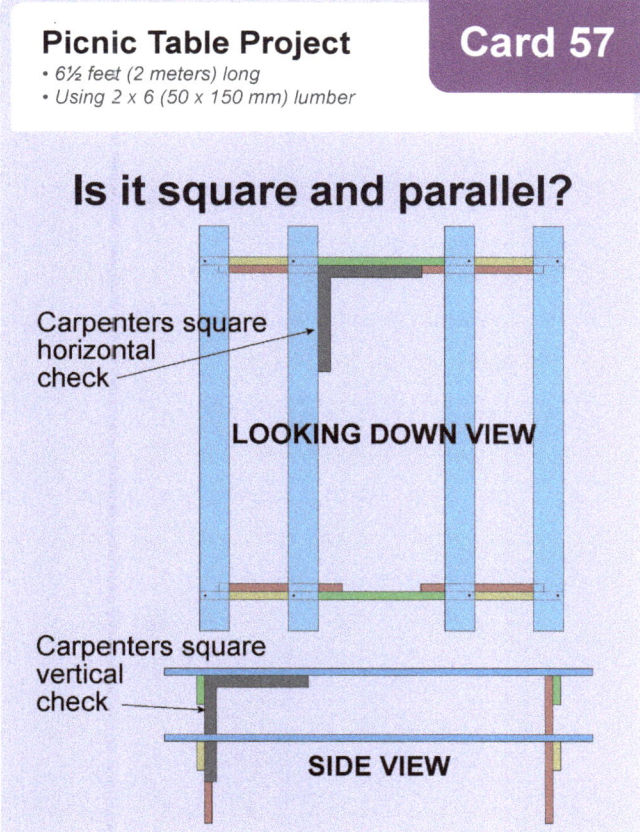

Carpenters square horizontal check

LOOKING DOWN VIEW

Carpenters square vertical check

SIDE VIEW

Picnic Table Project
Card 58
- 6½ feet (2 meters) long
- Using 2 x 6 (50 x 150 mm) lumber

Is it square and parallel? [explanation]

Check that the frames are parallel, and with a carpenter's square ensure the frames are square (at right angles) to the tabletop and seat boards, both horizontally and vertically. If necessary, make any straightening adjustments, then add a second screw to each joint.

This will hold the unit square while you continue to add the intermediate boards.

Picnic Table Project
Card 59
- 6½ feet (2 meters) long
- Using 2 x 6 (50 x 150 mm) lumber

Add the intermediate boards

Place the intermediate boards. Ensure the ends are flush and the gaps between the boards are even.

Draw a 'screw line' across the table and seats to keep the screws in a straight line.

Picnic Table Project
Card 60
- 6½ feet (2 meters) long
- Using 2 x 6 (50 x 150 mm) lumber

Screwing detail

Use 3½" (90 mm) exterior wood screws. Ensure the screws are in a straight line purely for aesthetic purposes.
Drill clearance holes through the top boards prior to screwing.

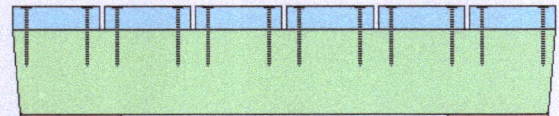

Picnic Table Project
- 6½ feet (2 meters) long
- Using 2 x 6 (50 x 150 mm) lumber

Card 61

Attach the cleats

With the table upside-down, screw cleats across the center of the seats and the tabletop.

Use two 3" (75 mm) screws positioned diagonally across each joint.

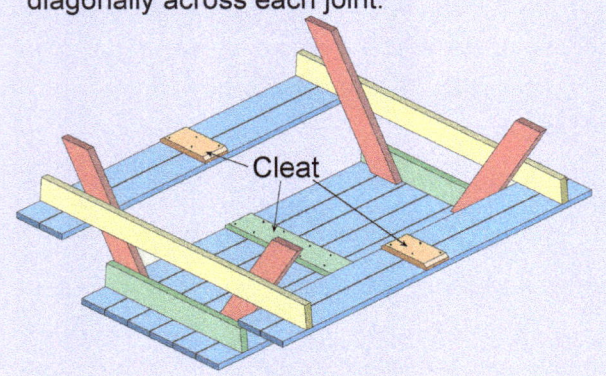

Picnic Table Project
- 6½ feet (2 meters) long
- Using 2 x 6 (50 x 150 mm) lumber

Card 62

Add bracing

Ensure the end-frames are square (upright) to the tabletop, and then position each brace as shown in the image below. Screw one end of the brace to the middle rail with two 3" (75 mm) screws, and the other end with 3 screws angled into the tabletop.

Picnic Table Project
- 6½ feet (2 meters) long
- Using 2 x 6 (50 x 150 mm) lumber

Card 63

Drill and bolt

Drill a bolt hole through the center of every leg and rail joint - eight altogether.

Insert 1/2" (12 mm) galvanised bolts, add washers and nuts, and tighten them up.

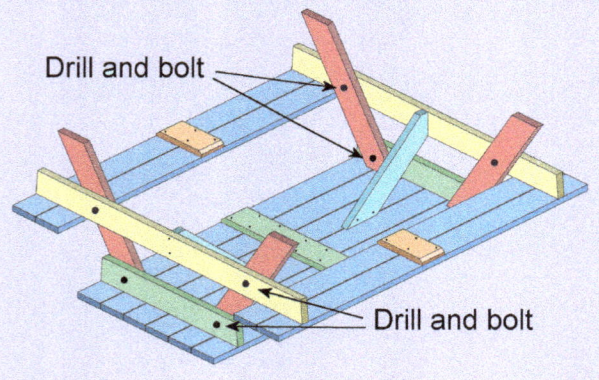

Picnic Table Project
- 6½ feet (2 meters) long
- Using 2 x 6 (50 x 150 mm) lumber

Card 64

All finished!

And there it is.

A nice solid, comfortable picnic table that will seat at least six people.

Enjoy!

You are now leaving the

6-1/2 feet (2 meters) long picnic table project

constructed out of

2 x 6 (50 x 150 mm) lumber

Next up

8 feet (2.4 meters) long picnic table project

using

2 x 4 (50 x 100 mm) lumber

Build your own Picnic Table

8 feet (2.4 meters) long

Using 2 x 4 (50 x 100 mm) lumber

It will comfortably seat 8 people

Just follow the cards →

Card 65

Build Your Own Picnic Table

* *8 feet (2.4 meters) long*
* *Using 2 x 4 (50 x 100 mm) lumber*

Just follow the cards

Card 66

Picnic Table Project
• 8 feet (2.4 meters) long
• Using 2 x 4 (50 x 100 mm) lumber

Description

This picnic table is constructed out of 2 x 4 (50 x 100 mm) lumber. It will comfortably seat 8 people. Wide seats positioned both in terms of height and distance from the tabletop ensures easy access and maximum comfort.

Dimensions:

- Length: 8 feet (2.4 m)
- Width: 67" (1700 mm)
- Height: 29⅞" (758 mm)
- Tabletop width: 34¼" (870 mm)

Card 67

Picnic Table Project
• 8 feet (2.4 meters) long
• Using 2 x 4 (50 x 100 mm) lumber

Table of Contents - 1

Description	Card 66
Part identification	Card 69
Plans: Imperial measurements	Card 70
Plans: Metric measurements	Card 71
About the measurements	Card 72
Shopping list: Lumber	Card 73
Shopping list: Fixings	Card 74
Cutting list	Card 76
Cut the components to length	Card 78
Cutting plan	Card 79

Card 68

Picnic Table Project
• 8 feet (2.4 meters) long
• Using 2 x 4 (50 x 100 mm) lumber

Table of Contents - 2

Cut the angled pieces	Card 80
Arrange the legs	Card 82
Assemble the frames	Card 83
Stand the frames	Card 85
Put on the outer boards	Card 87
Check for square and parallel	Card 89
Add the intermediate boards	Card 91
Attach the cleats	Card 93
Add bracing	Card 94
Drill and bolt	Card 95

Picnic Table Project — Card 69
- *8 feet (2.4 meters) long*
- *Using 2 x 4 (50 x 100 mm) lumber*

Part Identification

- [f] Seat cleat
- [g] Table cleat
- [h] Brace
- [d] Tabletop board
- [c] Top rail
- [a] Leg
- [b] Middle rail
- [e] Seat board

Picnic Table Project — Card 70
- *8 feet (2.4 meters) long*
- *Using 2 x 4 (50 x 100 mm) lumber*

Plans: Imperial measurements

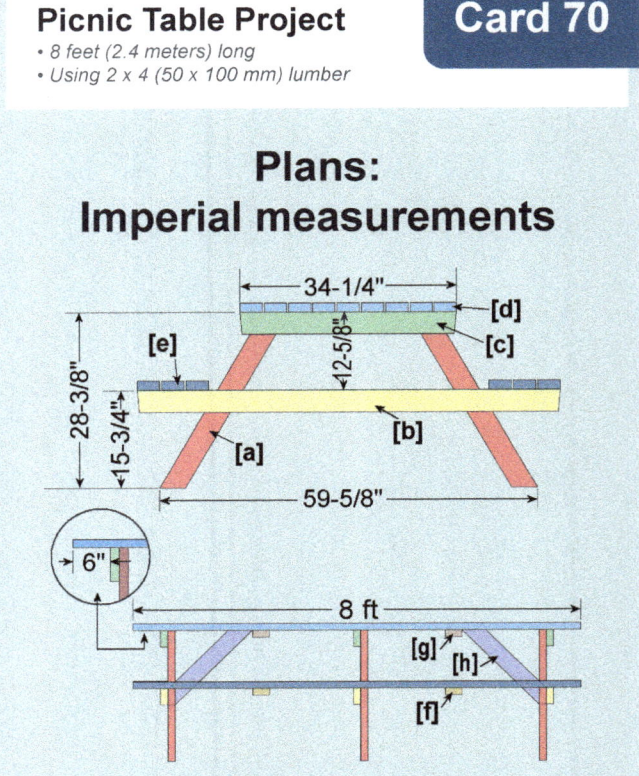

Picnic Table Project — Card 71
- *8 feet (2.4 meters) long*
- *Using 2 x 4 (50 x 100 mm) lumber*

Plans: Metric measurements

Picnic Table Project — Card 72
- *8 feet (2.4 meters) long*
- *Using 2 x 4 (50 x 100 mm) lumber*

About the measurements

Length measurements in this project are given in both imperial units (inches) and metric units (millimeters).

When the measurements are presented side by side, the inch measurements are given first followed by the metric equivalent in brackets.

For example: 15-3/4" (400 mm).

Card 73

Picnic Table Project
- 8 feet (2.4 meters) long
- Using 2 x 4 (50 x 100 mm) lumber

Shopping list: Lumber

Wood size	Length	Qty
2 x 4 (50 x 100 mm)	8 ft (2.4 m)	24

From the lengths provided above you will be able to cut all the pieces that are required to construct the picnic table.

Card 79 shows how you can cut all the pieces from the above lengths to minimize waste.

Card 74

Picnic Table Project
- 8 feet (2.4 meters) long
- Using 2 x 4 (50 x 100 mm) lumber

Shopping list: Fixings

Exterior wood screws:
- 118 screws 3" (75 mm) long.
- 90 screws 3½" (90 mm) long.

1/2" (12 mm) galvanized coach/carriage bolts:
- 12 bolts 4" (100 mm) long.
- 12 each nuts and washers to match.

Note: Use the 3" (75 mm) screws for the frames, cleats, and braces.

Use the 3½" (90 mm) screws for the seat boards and the tabletop boards.

Card 75

Picnic Table Project
- 8 feet (2.4 meters) long
- Using 2 x 4 (50 x 100 mm) lumber

Dressed lumber

Dressed lumber is wood that has been planed and smoothed, which makes it smaller than the nominal sizes given.

For example, 2 x 4 (50 x 100 mm) dressed lumber will be 1½" x 3½" (38 x 89 mm) in actual size.

Note: The difference in size will not impact the build, as it is the lengths of the pieces that are important, not so much the size (width and thickness) of the wood.

Card 76

Picnic Table Project
- 8 feet (2.4 meters) long
- Using 2 x 4 (50 x 100 mm) lumber

Cutting list

2 x 4 (50 x 100 mm) lumber		
Piece ID	Length	Qty
[a] Leg	34¾" (883 mm)	6
[b] Middle rail	67" (1700 mm)	3
[c] Top rail	34¼" (870 mm)	3
[d] Tabletop board	8 feet (2.4 m)	9
[e] Seat board	8 feet (2.4 m)	6
[f] Seat cleat	11¼" (285 mm)	4
[g] Table cleat	34¼" (870 mm)	2
[h] Brace	25" (635 mm)	2

Picnic Table Project
- *8 feet (2.4 meters) long*
- *Using 2 x 4 (50 x 100 mm) lumber*

Card 77

INSTRUCTIONS

Let's Go!

Start the build

Just follow the cards

Picnic Table Project
- *8 feet (2.4 meters) long*
- *Using 2 x 4 (50 x 100 mm) lumber*

Card 78

Cut all the pieces

All lumber is 2 x 4 (50 x 100 mm) stock.

Cut all the pieces to the lengths given in the 'Cutting List' (**Card 76**).

All the pieces can be cut from the standard stock lengths that are listed in the 'Shopping list' (**Card 79**).

Following on the next card is a plan drawing showing how all the pieces can be cut from the standard lengths of lumber given in the 'Shopping list'.

Picnic Table Project
- *8 feet (2.4 meters) long*
- *Using 2 x 4 (50 x 100 mm) lumber*

Card 79

Cutting plan

The drawing below demonstrates how to cut all the necessary components from 24 pieces of 2 x 4 (50 x 100 mm) lumber, each being 8 ft (2.4 m) long.

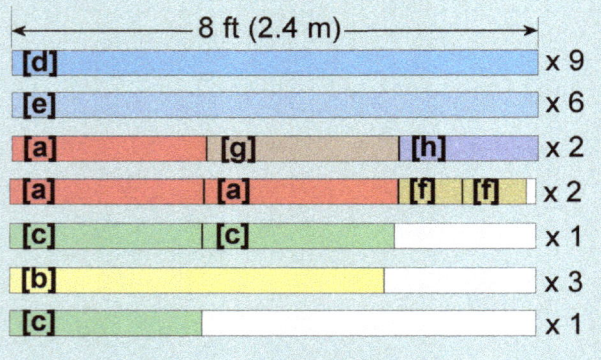

Picnic Table Project
- *8 feet (2.4 meters) long*
- *Using 2 x 4 (50 x 100 mm) lumber*

Card 80

Cut the angles pieces

Once all the pieces are cut to length, pieces **[a]**, **[b]**, **[c]**, and **[h]** need to have the ends cut at an angle. Cut the angles according to the drawings below.

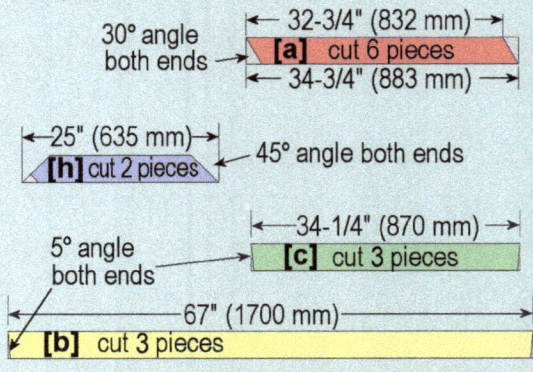

Picnic Table Project
- *8 feet (2.4 meters) long*
- *Using 2 x 4 (50 x 100 mm) lumber*

Card 81

Ready to assemble

At this stage, you should have all the pieces cut as shown below, ready for assembly.

- **[a]** Leg — 6 pieces
- **[b]** Middle rail — 3 pieces
- **[c]** Top rail — 3 pieces
- **[d]** Tabletop board — 9 pieces
- **[e]** Seat board — 6 pieces
- **[f]** Seat cleat — 4 pieces
- **[g]** Table cleat — 2 piece
- **[h]** Brace — 2 pieces

Picnic Table Project
- *8 feet (2.4 meters) long*
- *Using 2 x 4 (50 x 100 mm) lumber*

Card 82

Arrange the legs

Lay each pair of legs flat on an even surface, spaced according to the plan drawing below. Use a straight-edge to ensure the bottom of both legs are in-line.

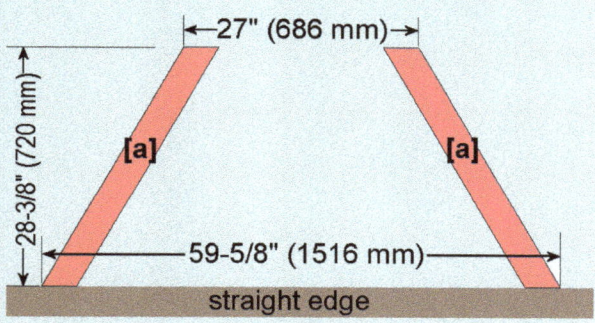

Picnic Table Project
- *8 feet (2.4 meters) long*
- *Using 2 x 4 (50 x 100 mm) lumber*

Card 83

Assemble the frames

Place cross rails **[b]** and **[c]** on legs **[a]** according to the plan drawing below. Use four 3" (75 mm) screws at each joint, as illustrated in the drawing below. Do not place screws in the middle of a joint, as that space is reserved for a bolt.

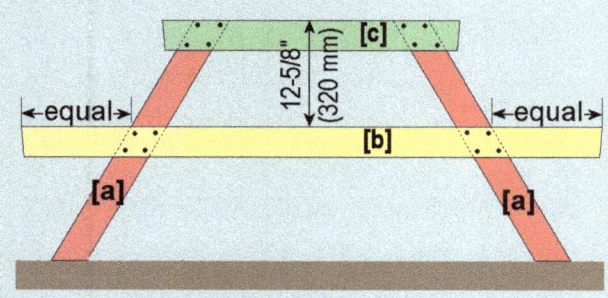

Picnic Table Project
- *8 feet (2.4 meters) long*
- *Using 2 x 4 (50 x 100 mm) lumber*

Card 84

Screwing

Whenever you're fastening two pieces of wood together with screws, it's important to predrill a **clearance hole** through the top piece.

A **clearance hole** should have the same diameter or slightly larger (but never smaller) than the outside diameter of the screw threads. This allows the screw to go through the top piece smoothly, with the threads only gripping into the bottom piece, ensuring a tight connection between the two parts.

Picnic Table Project
Card 85
- 8 feet (2.4 meters) long
- Using 2 x 4 (50 x 100 mm) lumber

Stand the frames

Clamp a block to each leg as illustrated in the drawing below. This allows the frames to stand independently. You can position the frames and place the boards without needing help from another person.

Picnic Table Project
Card 86
- 8 feet (2.4 meters) long
- Using 2 x 4 (50 x 100 mm) lumber

Arrange the frames

Now, evenly space the frames approximately so that when the tabletop and seat boards are positioned, they will overhang the frames at each end by 6" (150 mm).

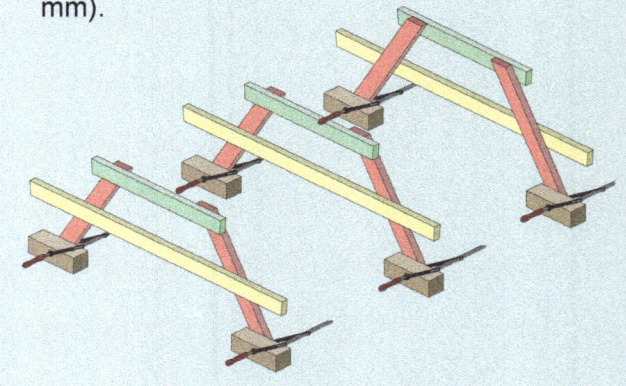

Picnic Table Project
Card 87
- 8 feet (2.4 meters) long
- Using 2 x 4 (50 x 100 mm) lumber

Put on the outer boards

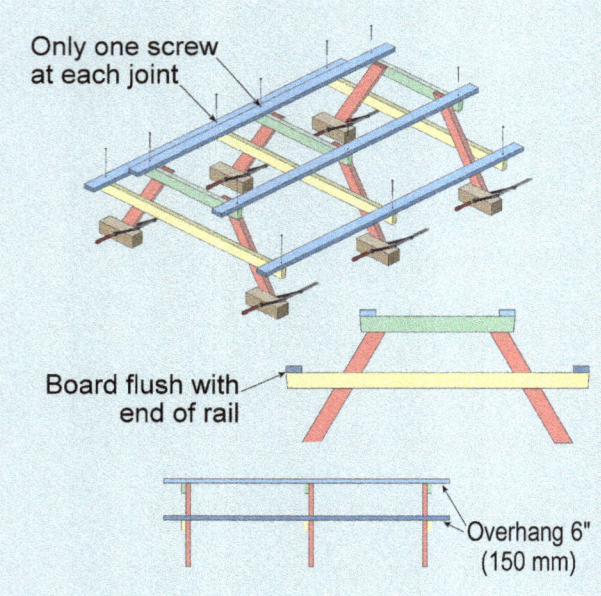

Only one screw at each joint

Board flush with end of rail

Overhang 6" (150 mm)

Picnic Table Project
Card 88
- 8 feet (2.4 meters) long
- Using 2 x 4 (50 x 100 mm) lumber

Put on the outer boards [explanation]

First, place the outer tabletop and seat boards onto the frame rails, having them overhang each end by 6" (150 mm). Refer to the drawing on the previous card for placement. Secure the boards with **only one screw** at each joint - for the time being. A second screw will be added when the frames have been checked square and parallel.

Use 3½" (90 mm) screws positioned ⅝" (15 mm) in from the edge of the board.

Picnic Table Project
Card 89
- 8 feet (2.4 meters) long
- Using 2 x 4 (50 x 100 mm) lumber

Is it square and parallel?

LOOKING DOWN VIEW

Carpenters square horizontal check

Carpenters square vertical check

SIDE VIEW

Picnic Table Project
Card 90
- 8 feet (2.4 meters) long
- Using 2 x 4 (50 x 100 mm) lumber

Is it square and parallel? [explanation]

Check that the frames are parallel, and with a carpenter's square ensure the frames are square (at right angles) to the tabletop and seat boards, both horizontally and vertically. If necessary, make any straightening adjustments, then add a second screw to each joint. This will hold the unit square while you continue to add the intermediate boards.

Picnic Table Project
Card 91
- 8 feet (2.4 meters) long
- Using 2 x 4 (50 x 100 mm) lumber

Add the intermediate boards

Place the intermediate boards. Ensure the ends are flush and the gaps between the boards are even.
Draw a 'screw line' across the table and the seats to keep the screws in a straight line.

Picnic Table Project
Card 92
- 8 feet (2.4 meters) long
- Using 2 x 4 (50 x 100 mm) lumber

Screwing detail

Use 3½" (90 mm) exterior wood screws.
Ensure the screws are in a straight line purely for aesthetic purposes.
Drill clearance holes through the boards prior to screwing.

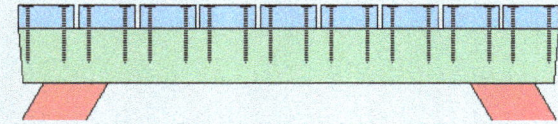

Picnic Table Project
- *8 feet (2.4 meters) long*
- *Using 2 x 4 (50 x 100 mm) lumber*

Card 93

Attach the cleats

With the table upside-down, screw cleats across the seats and the tabletop, centered between the frames. Use two 3" (75 mm) screws positioned diagonally across each joint.

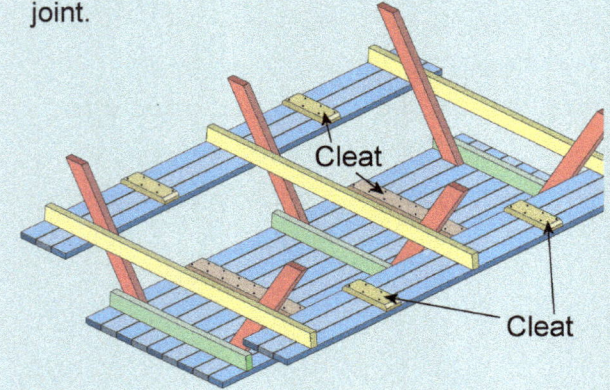

Picnic Table Project
- *8 feet (2.4 meters) long*
- *Using 2 x 4 (50 x 100 mm) lumber*

Card 94

Add bracing

Ensure the end-frames are square (upright) to the tabletop, and then position each brace as shown in the image below. Screw one end of the brace to the middle rail with two 3" (75 mm) screws, and the other end with 3 screws angled into the tabletop.

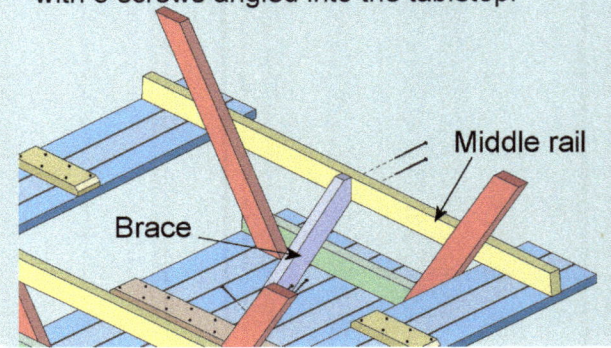

Picnic Table Project
- *8 feet (2.4 meters) long*
- *Using 2 x 4 (50 x 100 mm) lumber*

Card 95

Drill and bolt

Drill a bolt hole through the center of every leg and rail joint - twelve altogether. Insert 1/2" (12 mm) galvanised bolts, add washers and nuts, and tighten them up.

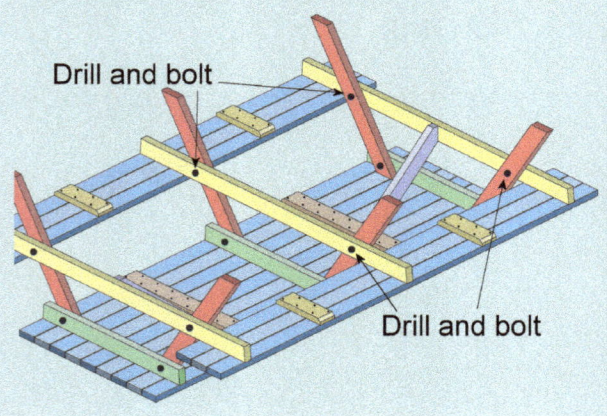

Picnic Table Project
- *8 feet (2.4 meters) long*
- *Using 2 x 4 (50 x 100 mm) lumber*

Card 96

All finished!

And there it is.
A nice solid, comfortable picnic table that will seat eight people.

Enjoy!

You are now leaving the
8 feet (2.4 meters) long picnic table project
constructed out of
2 x 4 (50 x 100 mm) lumber

Next up

8 feet (2.4 meters) long picnic table project
using
2 x 6 (50 x 150 mm) lumber

Build your own Picnic Table

8 feet (2.4 meters) long

Using 2 x 6 (50 x 150 mm) lumber

It will comfortably seat 8 people

Just follow the cards →

Card 97

Build Your Own Picnic Table

* *8 feet (2.4 meters) long*
* *Using 2 x 6 (50 x 150 mm) lumber*

Just follow the cards

Card 98

Picnic Table Project
* *8 feet (2.4 meters) long*
* *Using 2 x 6 (50 x 150 mm) lumber*

Description

This picnic table is constructed out of 2 x 6 (50 x 150 mm) lumber. It will comfortably seat 8 people. Wide seats positioned both in terms of height and distance from the tabletop ensures easy access and maximum comfort.

Dimensions:
- Length: 8 feet (2.4m)
- Width: 67" (1700 mm)
- Height: 29⅞" (758 mm)
- Tabletop width: 34¼" (870 mm)

Card 99

Picnic Table Project
* *8 feet (2.4 meters) long*
* *Using 2 x 6 (50 x 150 mm) lumber*

Table of Contents - 1

Description	Card 98
Part identification	Card 101
Plans: Imperial measurements	Card 102
Plans: Metric measurements	Card 103
About the measurements	Card 104
Shopping list: Lumber	Card 105
Shopping list: Fixings	Card 106
Cutting list	Card 108
Cut the components to length	Card 110
Cutting plan	Card 111

Card 100

Picnic Table Project
* *8 feet (2.4 meters) long*
* *Using 2 x 6 (50 x 150 mm) lumber*

Table of Contents - 2

Cut the angled pieces	Card 112
Arrange the legs	Card 114
Assemble the frames	Card 115
Stand the frames	Card 117
Put on the outer boards	Card 119
Check for square and parallel	Card 121
Add the intermediate boards	Card 123
Attach the cleats	Card 125
Add bracing	Card 126
Drill and bolt	Card 127

Picnic Table Project — 101
- *8 feet (2.4 meters) long*
- *Using 2 x 6 (50 x 150 mm) lumber*

Part Identification

[a] Leg; [b] Middle rail; [c] Top rail;
[d] Tabletop board; [e] Seat board;
[f] Seat cleat; [g] Table cleat;
[h] Brace;
[i] Brace support.

Picnic Table Project — Card 102
- *8 feet (2.4 meters) long*
- *Using 2 x 6 (50 x 150 mm) lumber*

Plans: Imperial measurements

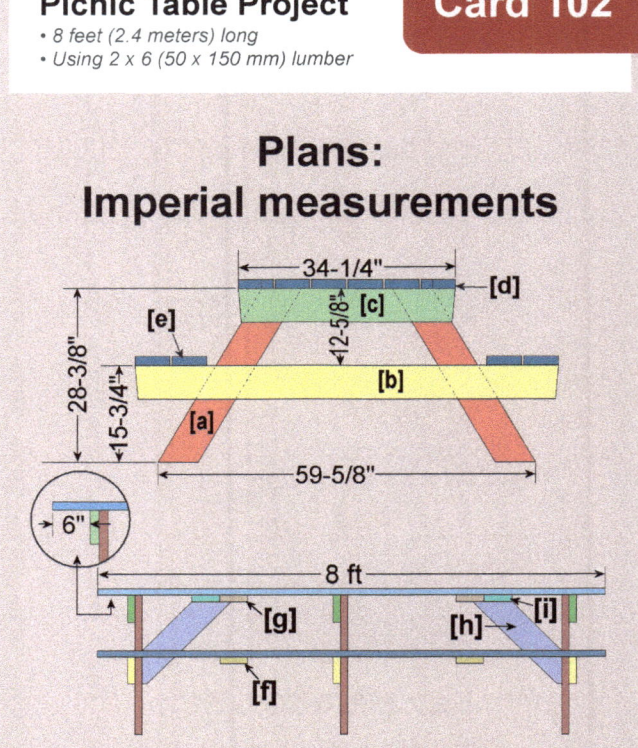

Picnic Table Project — Card 103
- *8 feet (2.4 meters) long*
- *Using 2 x 6 (50 x 150 mm) lumber*

Plans: Metric measurements

Picnic Table Project — Card 104
- *8 feet (2.4 meters) long*
- *Using 2 x 6 (50 x 150 mm) lumber*

About the measurements

Length measurements in this project are given in both imperial units (inches) and metric units (millimeters).

When the measurements are presented side by side, the inch measurements are given first followed by the metric equivalent in brackets.

For example: 15-3/4" (400 mm).

Card 105

Picnic Table Project
- *8 feet (2.4 meters) long*
- *Using 2 x 6 (50 x 150 mm) lumber*

Shopping list: Lumber

Wood size	Length	Qty
2 x 6 (50 x 150 mm)	8 ft (2.4 m)	19

The lengths provided above are standard stock sizes.
From those lengths you will be able to cut all the pieces that are required to construct the picnic table.

Card 111 shows how you can cut all the pieces from the above lengths to minimize waste.

Card 106

Picnic Table Project
- *8 feet (2.4 meters) long*
- *Using 2 x 6 (50 x 150 mm) lumber*

Shopping list: Fixings

Exterior wood screws:
- 106 screws 3" (75 mm) long.
- 60 screws 3½" (90 mm) long.

1/2" (12 mm) galvanized coach/carriage bolts:
- 12 bolts 4½" (120 mm) long.
- 12 each nuts and washers to match.

Note: Use the 3" (75 mm) screws for the frames, cleats, braces, and brace supports.

Use the 3½" (90 mm) screws for the seat boards and the tabletop boards.

Card 107

Picnic Table Project
- *8 feet (2.4 meters) long*
- *Using 2 x 6 (50 x 150 mm) lumber*

Dressed lumber

Dressed lumber is wood that has been planed and smoothed, which makes it smaller than the nominal sizes given.

For example, 2 x 6 (50 x 150 mm) dressed lumber will be 1½" x 5½" (38 x 140 mm) in actual size.

Note: The difference in size will not impact the build, as it is the lengths of the pieces that are important, not so much the size (width and thickness) of the wood.

Card 108

Picnic Table Project
- *8 feet (2.4 meters) long*
- *Using 2 x 6 (50 x 150 mm) lumber*

Cutting list

2 x 6 (50 x 150 mm) lumber		
Piece ID	Length	Qty
[a] Leg	36" (912 mm)	6
[b] Middle rail	67" (1700 mm)	3
[c] Top rail	34¼" (870 mm)	3
[d] Tabletop board	8 feet (2.4 m)	6
[e] Seat board	8 feet (2.4 m)	4
[f] Seat cleat	11¼" (285 mm)	4
[g] Table cleat	34¼" (870 mm)	2
[h] Brace	27" (686 mm)	2
[i] Brace support	11¼" (286 mm)	2

Card 109

Picnic Table Project
- *8 feet (2.4 meters) long*
- *Using 2 x 6 (50 x 150 mm) lumber*

INSTRUCTIONS

Let's Go!

Start the build

Just follow the cards

Card 110

Picnic Table Project
- *8 feet (2.4 meters) long*
- *Using 2 x 6 (50 x 150 mm) lumber*

Cut all the pieces

All lumber is 2 x 6 (50 x 150 mm) stock.

Cut all the pieces to the lengths given in the 'Cutting list' (**Card 108**).

All the pieces can be cut from the standard stock lengths that are listed in the 'Shopping list' (**Card 105**).

Following on the next card is a plan drawing showing how all the pieces can be cut from the standard lengths of lumber given in the 'Shopping list'.

Card 111

Picnic Table Project
- *8 feet (2.4 meters) long*
- *Using 2 x 6 (50 x 150 mm) lumber*

Cutting plan

The drawing below illustrates how all the necessary pieces can be cut from nineteen lengths of 2 x 6 (50 x 150 mm) lumber, each measuring 8 feet (2.4m) in length.

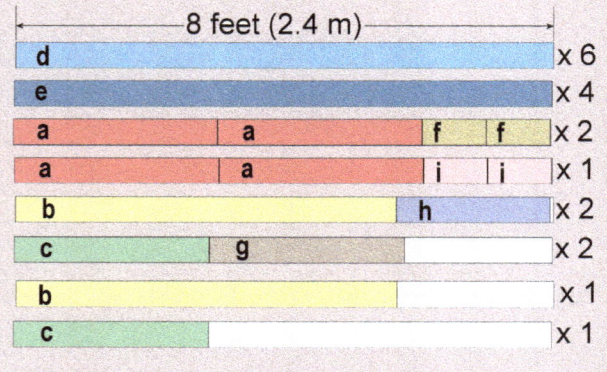

Card 112

Picnic Table Project
- *8 feet (2.4 meters) long*
- *Using 2 x 6 (50 x 150 mm) lumber*

Cut the angles pieces

Once all the pieces are cut to length, pieces **[a]**, **[b]**, **[c]**, and **[h]** need to have the ends cut at an angle. Cut the angles according to the drawings below.

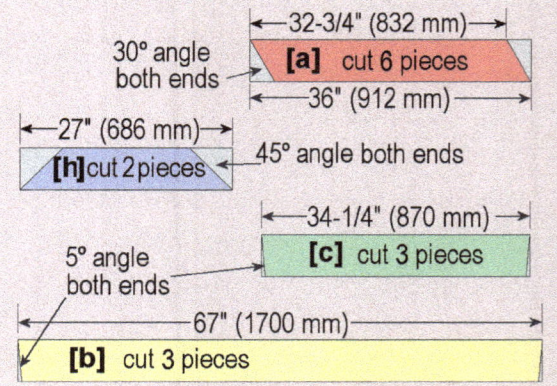

Picnic Table Project — Card 113
- 8 feet (2.4 meters) long
- Using 2 x 6 (50 x 150 mm) lumber

Ready to assemble

At this stage, you should have all the pieces cut as shown below, ready for assembly.

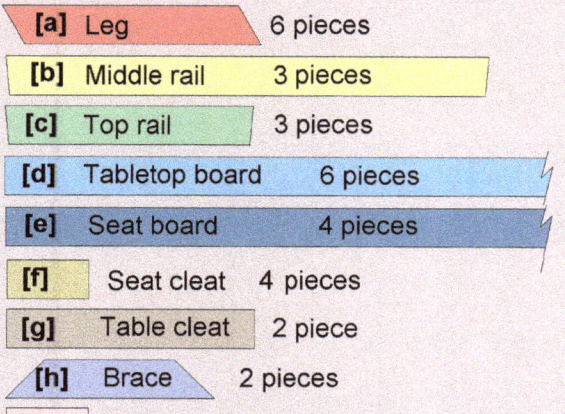

- [a] Leg — 6 pieces
- [b] Middle rail — 3 pieces
- [c] Top rail — 3 pieces
- [d] Tabletop board — 6 pieces
- [e] Seat board — 4 pieces
- [f] Seat cleat — 4 pieces
- [g] Table cleat — 2 piece
- [h] Brace — 2 pieces
- [f] Brace support — 2 pieces

Picnic Table Project — Card 114
- 8 feet (2.4 meters) long
- Using 2 x 6 (50 x 150 mm) lumber

Arrange the legs

Lay each pair of legs flat on an even surface, spaced according to the plan drawing below. Use a straight-edge to ensure the bottom of both legs are in-line.

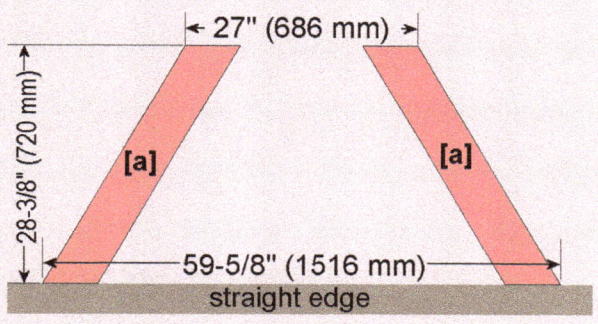

Picnic Table Project — Card 115
- 8 feet (2.4 meters) long
- Using 2 x 6 (50 x 150 mm) lumber

Assemble the frames

Place cross rails [b] and [c] on legs [a] according to the plan drawing below.
Use four 3" (75 mm) screws at each joint, as illustrated in the drawing below. Do not place screws in the middle of a joint, as that space is reserved for a bolt.

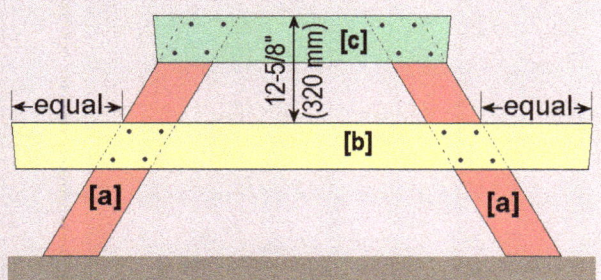

Picnic Table Project — Card 116
- 8 feet (2.4 meters) long
- Using 2 x 6 (50 x 150 mm) lumber

💡 Screwing

Whenever you're fastening two pieces of wood together with screws, it's important to predrill a **clearance hole** through the top piece.

A **clearance hole** should have the same diameter or slightly larger (but never smaller) than the outside diameter of the screw threads. This allows the screw to go through the top piece smoothly, with the threads only gripping into the bottom piece, ensuring a tight connection between the two parts.

Picnic Table Project
- 8 feet (2.4 meters) long
- Using 2 x 6 (50 x 150 mm) lumber

Card 117

Stand the frames

Clamp a block to flush to the bottom of each leg. This allows the frames to stand independently without needing help from another person to hold the frames upright.

Picnic Table Project
- 8 feet (2.4 meters) long
- Using 2 x 6 (50 x 150 mm) lumber

Card 118

Arrange the frames

Now, space the frames parallel and evenly apart so that when the tabletop and seat boards are positioned, they will overhang the frames at each end by 6" (150 mm).

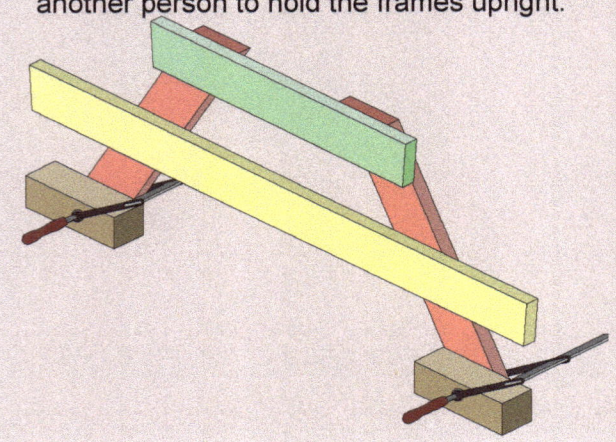
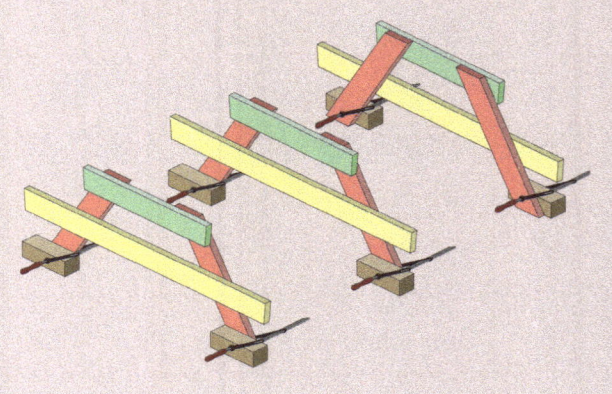

Picnic Table Project
- 8 feet (2.4 meters) long
- Using 2 x 6 (50 x 150 mm) lumber

Card 119

Put on the outer boards

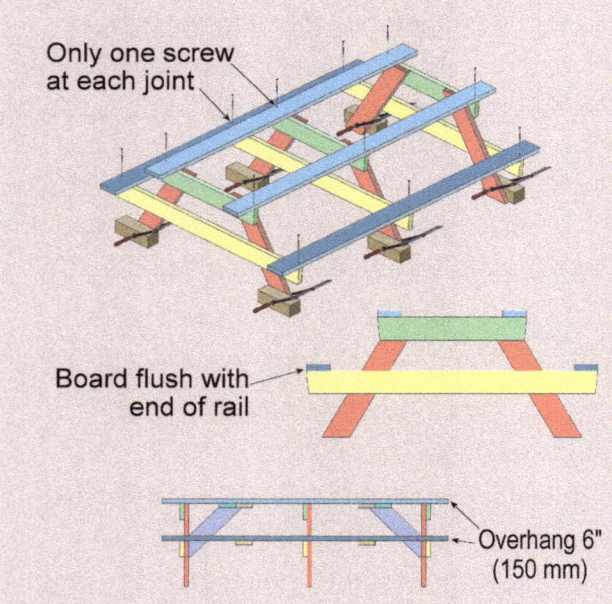

Only one screw at each joint

Board flush with end of rail

Overhang 6" (150 mm)

Picnic Table Project
- 8 feet (2.4 meters) long
- Using 2 x 6 (50 x 150 mm) lumber

Card 120

Put on the outer boards [explanation]

First, place the outer tabletop and seat boards onto the frame rails, having them overhang each end by 6" (150 mm). Refer to the drawing on the previous card for placement. Secure the boards **with only one screw** at each joint - for the time being. A second screw will be added when the frames have been checked square and parallel.

Use 3½" (90 mm) screws positioned 5/8" (15 mm) in from the edge of the board.

Picnic Table Project
Card 121
- 8 feet (2.4 meters) long
- Using 2 x 6 (50 x 150 mm) lumber

Is it square and parallel?

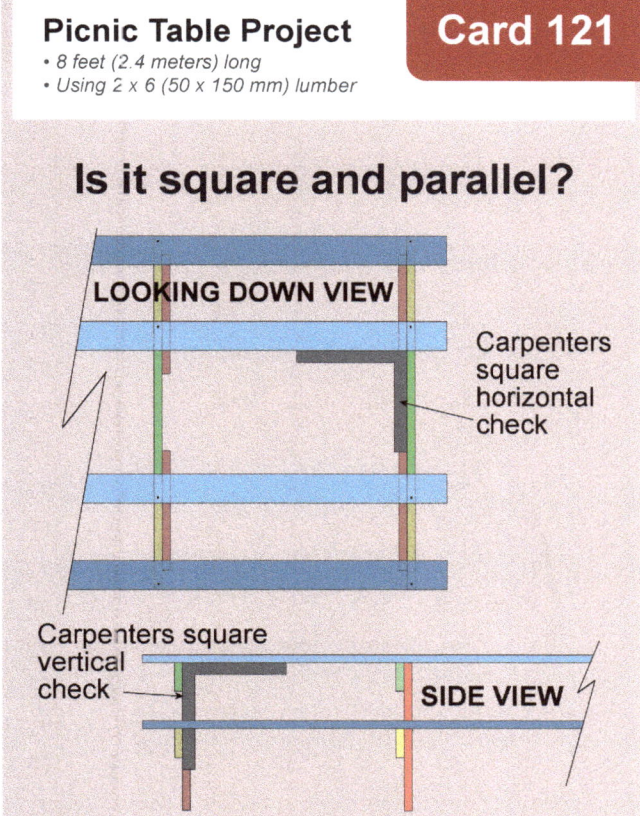

Picnic Table Project
Card 122
- 8 feet (2.4 meters) long
- Using 2 x 6 (50 x 150 mm) lumber

Is it square and parallel? [explanation]

Check that the frames are parallel and using a carpenter's square, ensure the frames are square to the tabletop and seat boards, both horizontally and vertically. If necessary, make any straightening adjustments. Then, add a second screw to each joint. This will hold the unit square while you continue to add the intermediate boards.

Picnic Table Project
Card 123
- 8 feet (2.4 meters) long
- Using 2 x 6 (50 x 150 mm) lumber

Add the intermediate boards

Place the intermediate boards. Ensure the ends are flush and the gaps between the boards are even.

Draw a 'screw line' across both the table and the seats to keep the screws in a straight line.

Picnic Table Project
Card 124
- 8 feet (2.4 meters) long
- Using 2 x 6 (50 x 150 mm) lumber

Screwing detail

Use 3½" (90 mm) exterior wood screws. Ensure the screws are in a straight line purely for aesthetic purposes.
Drill clearance holes through the boards prior to screwing.

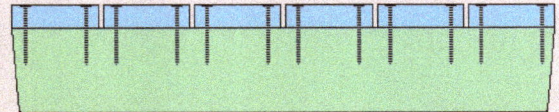

Picnic Table Project
Card 125
- 8 feet (2.4 meters) long
- Using 2 x 6 (50 x 150 mm) lumber

Attach the cleats

With the table upside-down, screw cleats across the seats and the tabletop, centered between the frames. Add the brace-support pieces **[i]** against the outer side of the seat cleats centered across the tabletop.

Use two 3" (75 mm) screws positioned diagonally across each joint.

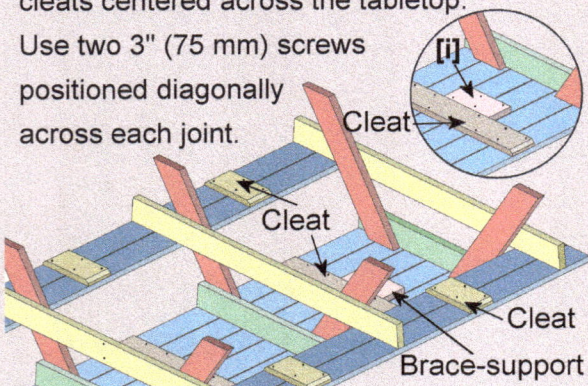

Picnic Table Project
Card 126
- 8 feet (2.4 meters) long
- Using 2 x 6 (50 x 150 mm) lumber

Add bracing

Ensure the end-frames are square (upright) to the tabletop, then position and screw each brace as shown in the image below.

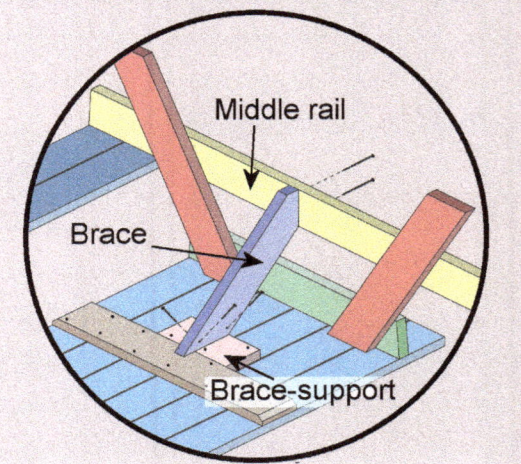

Picnic Table Project
Card 127
- 8 feet (2.4 meters) long
- Using 2 x 6 (50 x 150 mm) lumber

Drill and bolt

Drill a bolt hole through the center of every leg and rail joint - twelve altogether.

Insert 1/2" (12 mm) galvanised bolts, add washers and nuts, and tighten them up.

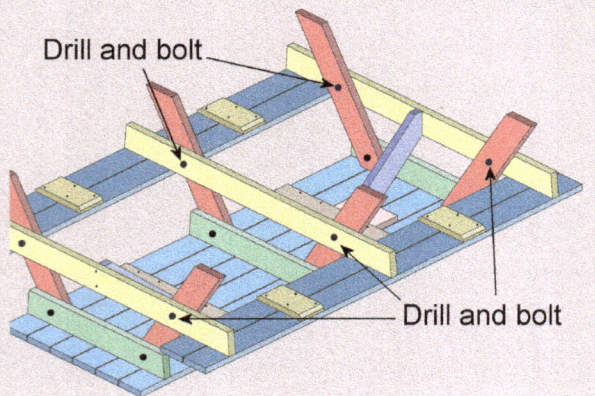

Picnic Table Project
Card 128
- 8 feet (2.4 meters) long
- Using 2 x 6 (50 x 150 mm) lumber

All finished!

And there it is.

A nice solid, comfortable picnic table that will seat eight people.

Enjoy!

You are now leaving the

8 feet (2.4 meters) long picnic table project

constructed out of

2 x 6 (50 x 150 mm) lumber

Next up

10 feet (3 meters) long picnic table project

using

2 x 4 (50 x 100 mm) lumber

Build your own Picnic Table

10 feet (3 meters) long

Using 2 x 4 (50 x 100 mm) lumber

It will comfortably seat 10 people

Just follow the cards →

Card 129

Build Your Own Picnic Table

* *10 feet (3 meters) long*
* *Using 2 x 4 (50 x 100 mm) lumber*

Just follow the cards

Card 130

Picnic Table Project
• *10 feet (3 meters) long*
• *Using 2 x 4 (50 x 100 mm) lumber*

Description

This picnic table is constructed out of 2 x 4 (50 x 100 mm) lumber. It will comfortably seat 10 people. Wide seats positioned both in terms of height and distance from the tabletop ensures easy access and maximum comfort.

Dimensions:

- Length: 10 feet (3 m)
- Width: 67" (1700 mm)
- Height: 29⅞" (758 mm)
- Tabletop width: 34¼" (870 mm)

Card 131

Picnic Table Project
• *10 feet (3 meters) long*
• *Using 2 x 4 (50 x 100 mm) lumber*

Table of Contents - 1

Description	Card 130
Part identification	Card 133
Plans: Imperial measurements	Card 134
Plans: Metric measurements	Card 135
About the measurements	Card 136
Shopping list: Lumber	Card 137
Shopping list: Fixings	Card 138
Cutting list	Card 140
Cut the components to length	Card 142
Cutting plan	Card 143

Card 132

Picnic Table Project
• *10 feet (3 meters) long*
• *Using 2 x 4 (50 x 100 mm) lumber*

Table of Contents - 2

Cut the angled pieces	Card 144
Arrange the legs	Card 146
Assemble the frames	Card 147
Stand the frames	Card 149
Put on the outer boards	Card 151
Check for square and parallel	Card 153
Add the intermediate boards	Card 155
Attach the cleats	Card 157
Add bracing	Card 158
Drill and bolt	Card 159

Picnic Table Project — Card 133
- *10 feet (3 meters) long*
- *Using 2 x 4 (50 x 100 mm) lumber*

Part Identification

- **[a]** Leg
- **[b]** Middle rail
- **[c]** Top rail
- **[d]** Tabletop board
- **[e]** Seat board
- **[f]** Seat cleat
- **[g]** Table cleat
- **[h]** Brace

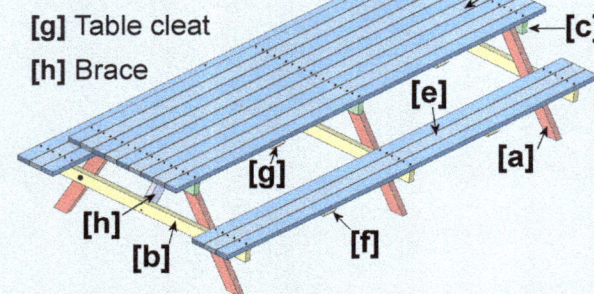

Picnic Table Project — Card 134
- *10 feet (3 meters) long*
- *Using 2 x 4 (50 x 100 mm) lumber*

Plans: Imperial measurements

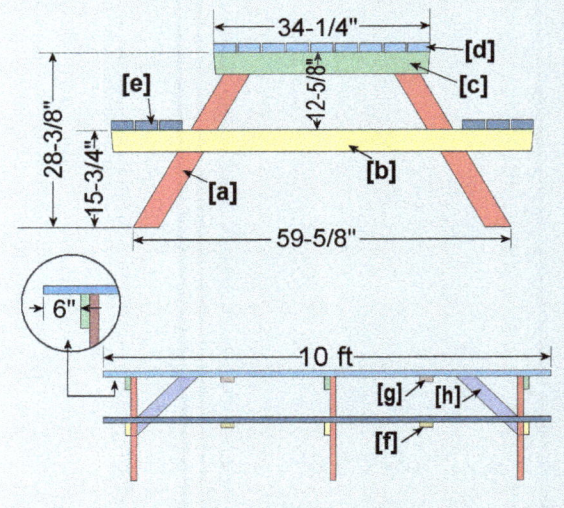

Picnic Table Project — Card 135
- *10 feet (3 meters) long*
- *Using 2 x 4 (50 x 100 mm) lumber*

Plans: Metric measurements

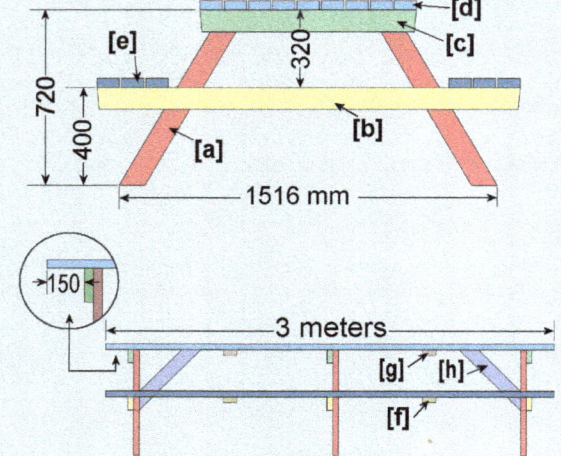

Picnic Table Project — Card 136
- *10 feet (3 meters) long*
- *Using 2 x 4 (50 x 100 mm) lumber*

About the measurements

Length measurements in this project are given in both imperial units (inches) and metric units (millimeters).

When the measurements are presented side by side, the inch measurements are given first followed by the metric equivalent in brackets.

For example: 15-3/4" (400 mm).

Picnic Table Project
- *10 feet (3 meters) long*
- *Using 2 x 4 (50 x 100 mm) lumber*

Card 137

Shopping list: Lumber

Wood size	Length	Qty
2 x 4 (50 x 100 mm)	10 ft (3 m)	21

The lengths provided above are standard stock sizes.

From those lengths you will be able to cut all the pieces that are required to construct the picnic table.

Card 143 shows how you can cut all the pieces from the above lengths to minimize waste.

Picnic Table Project
- *10 feet (3 meters) long*
- *Using 2 x 4 (50 x 100 mm) lumber*

Card 138

Shopping list: Fixings

Exterior wood screws:
- 118 screws 3" (75 mm) long.
- 90 screws 3½" (90 mm) long.

1/2" (12 mm) galvanized coach/carriage bolts:
- 12 bolts 4" (100 mm) long.
- 12 each nuts and washers to match.

Note: Use the 3" (75 mm) screws for the frames, cleats, and braces.
Use the 3½" (90 mm) screws for the seat boards and the tabletop boards.

Picnic Table Project
- *10 feet (3 meters) long*
- *Using 2 x 4 (50 x 100 mm) lumber*

Card 139

Dressed lumber

Dressed lumber is wood that has been planed and smoothed, which makes it smaller than the nominal sizes given.

For example, 2 x 4 (50 x 100 mm) dressed lumber will be 1½" x 3½" (38 x 89 mm) in actual size.

Note: The difference in size will not impact the build, as it is the lengths of the pieces that are important, not so much the size (width and thickness) of the wood.

Picnic Table Project
- *10 feet (3 meters) long*
- *Using 2 x 4 (50 x 100 mm) lumber*

Card 140

Cutting list

2 x 4 (50 x 100 mm) lumber		
Piece ID	Length	Qty
[a] Leg	34¾" (883 mm)	6
[b] Middle rail	67" (1700 mm)	3
[c] Top rail	34¼" (870 mm)	3
[d] Tabletop board	10 feet (3 m)	9
[e] Seat board	10 feet (3 m)	6
[f] Seat cleat	11¼" (285 mm)	4
[g] Table cleat	34¼" (870 mm)	2
[h] Brace	25" (635 mm)	2

Picnic Table Project
Card 141
- *10 feet (3 meters) long*
- *Using 2 x 4 (50 x 100 mm) lumber*

INSTRUCTIONS

Let's Go!

Start the build

Just follow the cards

Picnic Table Project
Card 142
- *10 feet (3 meters) long*
- *Using 2 x 4 (50 x 100 mm) lumber*

Cut all the pieces

All lumber is 2 x 4 (50 x 100 mm) stock.

Cut all the pieces to the lengths given in the 'Cutting List' (**Card 140**).

All the pieces can be cut from the standard stock lengths that are listed in the 'Shopping list' (**Card 137**).

Following on the next card is a plan drawing showing how all the pieces can be cut from the standard lengths of lumber given in the 'Shopping list'.

Picnic Table Project
Card 143
- *10 feet (3 meters) long*
- *Using 2 x 4 (50 x 100 mm) lumber*

Cutting plan

The drawing below demonstrates how to cut all the necessary components from twenty-one pieces of 2 x 4 (50 x 100 mm) lumber, each being 10 ft (3 m) long.

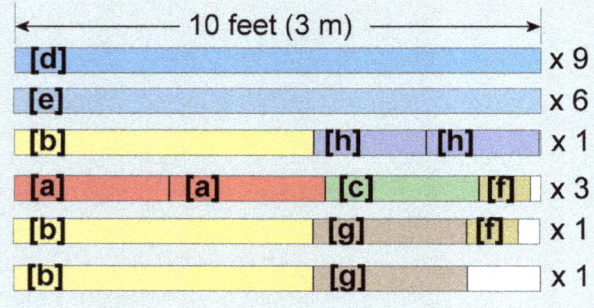

Picnic Table Project
Card 144
- *10 feet (3 meters) long*
- *Using 2 x 4 (50 x 100 mm) lumber*

Cut the angles pieces

Once all the pieces are cut to length, pieces **[a]**, **[b]**, **[c]**, and **[h]** need to have the ends cut at an angle. Cut the angles according to the drawings below.

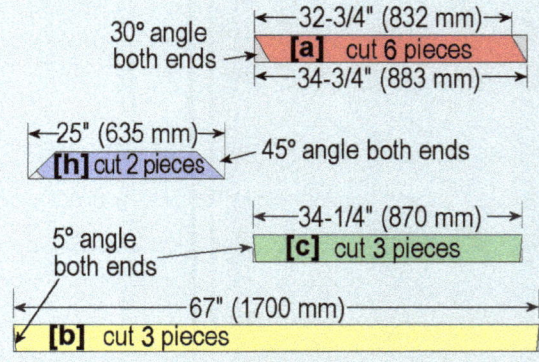

Picnic Table Project
- 10 feet (3 meters) long
- Using 2 x 4 (50 x 100 mm) lumber

Card 145

Ready to assemble

At this stage, you should have all the pieces cut as shown below, ready for assembly.

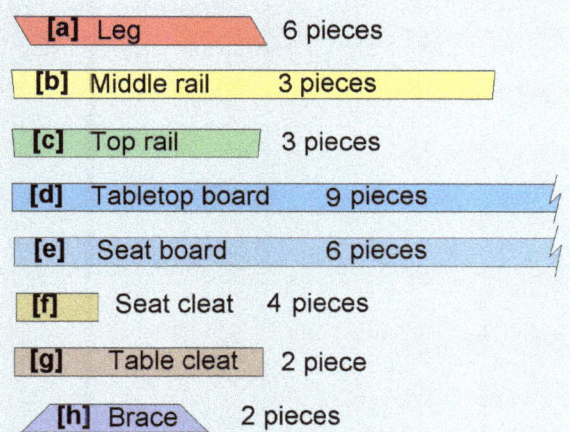

- [a] Leg — 6 pieces
- [b] Middle rail — 3 pieces
- [c] Top rail — 3 pieces
- [d] Tabletop board — 9 pieces
- [e] Seat board — 6 pieces
- [f] Seat cleat — 4 pieces
- [g] Table cleat — 2 piece
- [h] Brace — 2 pieces

Picnic Table Project
- 10 feet (3 meters) long
- Using 2 x 4 (50 x 100 mm) lumber

Card 146

Arrange the legs

Lay each pair of legs flat on an even surface, spaced according to the plan drawing below. Use a straight-edge to ensure the bottom of both legs are in-line.

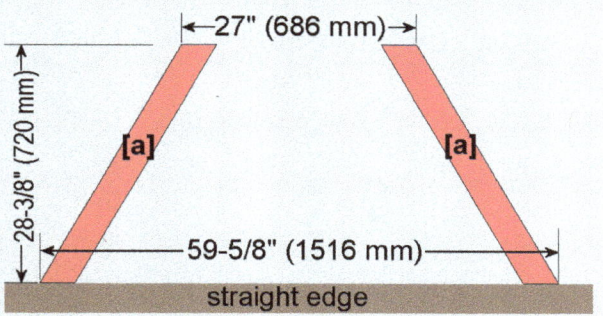

Picnic Table Project
- 10 feet (3 meters) long
- Using 2 x 4 (50 x 100 mm) lumber

Card 147

Assemble the frames

Place cross rails [b] and [c] on legs [a] according to the plan drawing below. Use four 3" (75 mm) screws at each joint, as illustrated in the drawing below. Do not place screws in the middle of a joint, as that space is reserved for a bolt.

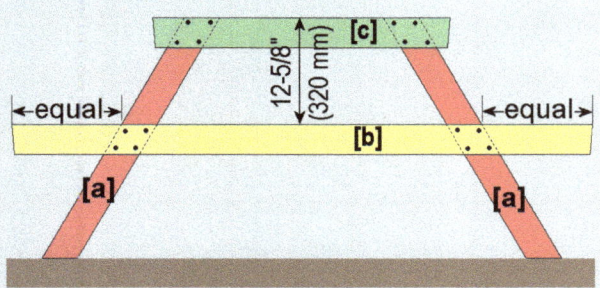

Picnic Table Project
- 10 feet (3 meters) long
- Using 2 x 4 (50 x 100 mm) lumber

Card 148

 ### Screwing

Whenever you're fastening two pieces of wood together with screws, it's important to predrill a **clearance hole** through the top piece.

A **clearance hole** should have the same diameter or slightly larger (but never smaller) than the outside diameter of the screw threads. This allows the screw to go through the top piece smoothly, with the threads only gripping into the bottom piece, ensuring a tight connection between the two parts.

Picnic Table Project
Card 149
- 10 feet (3 meters) long
- Using 2 x 4 (50 x 100 mm) lumber

Stand the frames

Clamp a block flush to the bottom of each leg, as illustrated in the drawing below. This will allow the frames to stand by themselves. Hence, you can position the frames and place the boards without needing help from another person to hold the frames upright.

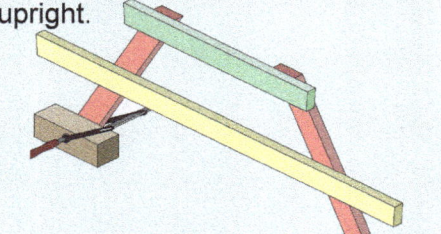

Picnic Table Project
Card 150
- 10 feet (3 meters) long
- Using 2 x 4 (50 x 100 mm) lumber

Arrange the frames

Now, evenly space the frames approximately so that when the tabletop and seat boards are positioned, they will overhang the frames at each end by 6" (150 mm).

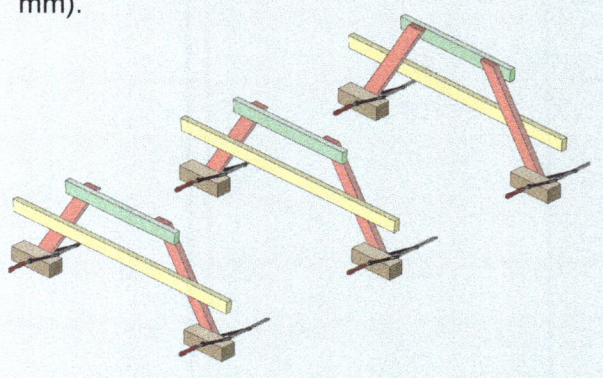

Picnic Table Project
Card 151
- 10 feet (3 meters) long
- Using 2 x 4 (50 x 100 mm) lumber

Put on the outer boards

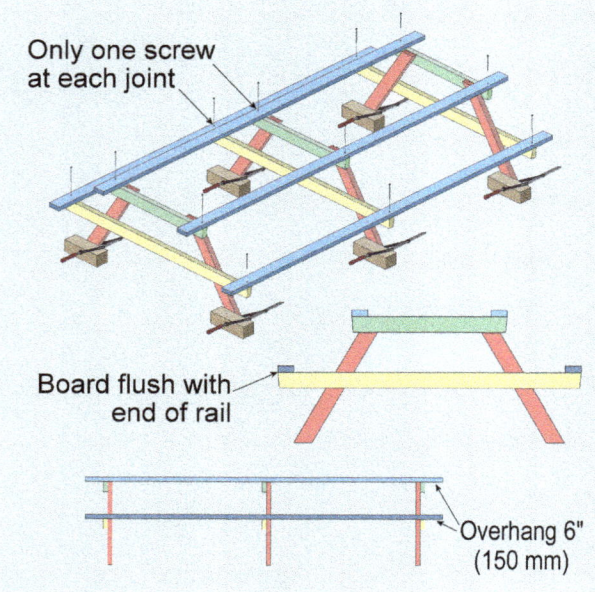

Picnic Table Project
Card 152
- 10 feet (3 meters) long
- Using 2 x 4 (50 x 100 mm) lumber

Put on the outer boards [explanation]

First, place the outer tabletop and seat boards onto the frame rails, having them overhang each end by 6" (150 mm). Refer to the drawing on the previous card for placement. Secure the boards with **only one screw** at each joint - for the time being. A second screw will be added when the frames have been checked square and parallel.

Use 3½" (90 mm) screws positioned ⅝" (15 mm) in from the outside edge of the board.

Picnic Table Project — Card 153
- 10 feet (3 meters) long
- Using 2 x 4 (50 x 100 mm) lumber

Is it square and parallel?

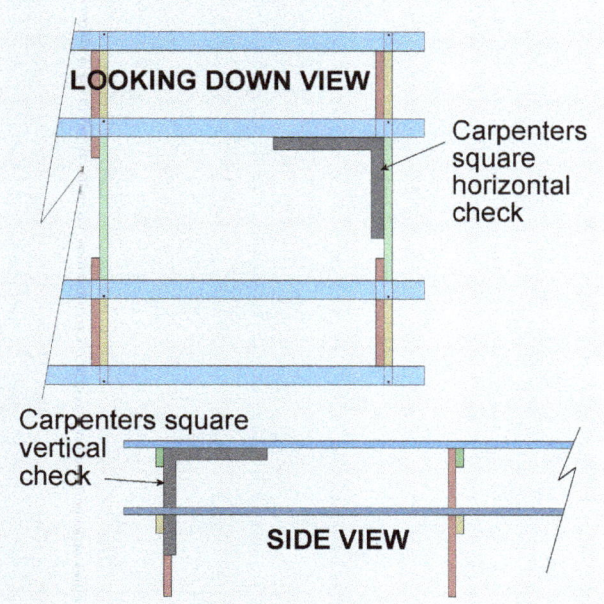

Picnic Table Project — Card 154
- 10 feet (3 meters) long
- Using 2 x 4 (50 x 100 mm) lumber

Is it square and parallel? [explanation]

Check that the frames are parallel and using a carpenter's square, ensure the frames are square to the tabletop and seat boards, both horizontally and vertically. If necessary, make any straightening adjustments. Then, add a second screw to each joint. This will hold the unit square while you continue to add the intermediate boards.

Picnic Table Project — Card 155
- 10 feet (3 meters) long
- Usirg 2 x 4 (50 x 100 mm) lumber

Add the intermediate boards

Place the intermediate boards. Ensure the ends are flush and the gaps between the boards are even.

Draw a 'screw line ' across both the table and the seats to keep the screws in a straight line.

Picnic Table Project — Card 156
- 10 feet (3 meters) long
- Using 2 x 4 (50 x 100 mm) lumber

Screwing detail

Use 3½" (90 mm) exterior wood screws. Ensure the screws are in a straight line.

Drill clearance holes through the boards prior to screwing.

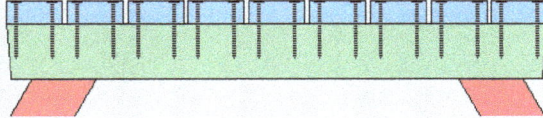

Picnic Table Project — Card 157
- *10 feet (3 meters) long*
- *Using 2 x 4 (50 x 100 mm) lumber*

Attach the cleats

With the table upside-down, screw cleats across the seats and the tabletop, centered between the frames. Use two 3" (75 mm) screws positioned diagonally across each joint.

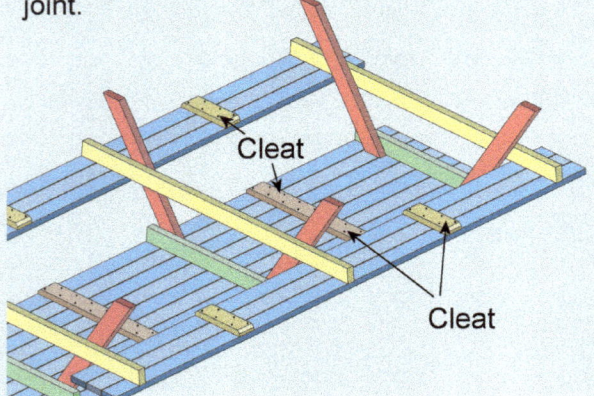

Picnic Table Project — Card 158
- *10 feet (3 meters) long*
- *Using 2 x 4 (50 x 100 mm) lumber*

Add bracing

Ensure the end-frames are square (upright) to the tabletop, and then position each brace as shown in the image below. Screw one end of the brace to the middle rail with two 3" (75 mm) screws, and the other end with 3 screws angled into the tabletop.

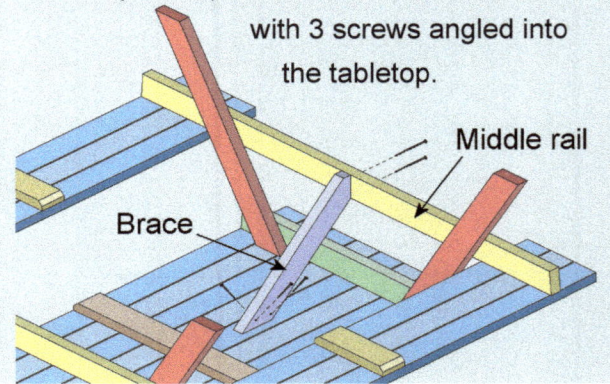

Picnic Table Project — Card 159
- *10 feet (3 meters) long*
- *Using 2 x 4 (50 x 100 mm) lumber*

Drill and bolt

Drill a bolt hole through the center of every leg and rail joint - twelve altogether. Make the holes slightly bigger than the diameter of the bolts. Insert 1/2" (12 mm) galvanised bolts, add washers and nuts, and tighten them up.

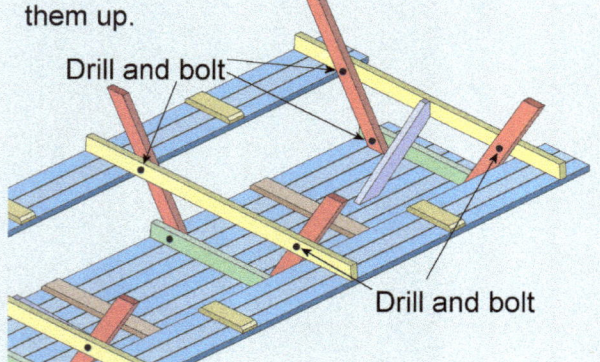

Picnic Table Project — Card 160
- *10 feet (3 meters) long*
- *Using 2 x 4 (50 x 100 mm) lumber*

All finished!

And there it is.
A nice solid, comfortable picnic table that will seat ten people.

Enjoy!

You are now leaving the

10 feet (3 meters) long picnic table project

constructed out of

2 x 4 (50 x 100 mm) lumber

Next up

10 feet (3 meters) long picnic table project

using

2 x 6 (50 x 150 mm) lumber

Build your own Picnic Table

10 feet (3 meters) long

Using 2 x 6 (50 x 150 mm) lumber

It will comfortably seat 10 people

Just follow the cards →

Card 161

Build Your Own Picnic Table

* *10 feet (3 meters) long*
* *Using 2 x 6 (50 x 150 mm) lumber*

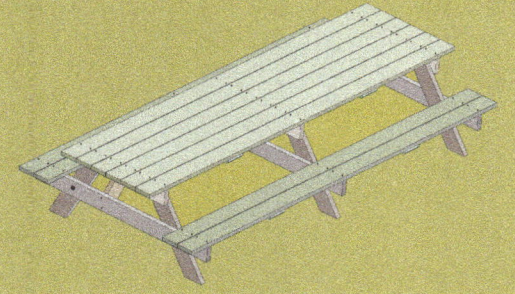

Just follow the cards

Card 162

Picnic Table Project
• *10 feet (3 meters) long*
• *Using 2 x 6 (50 x 150 mm) lumber*

Description

This picnic table is constructed out of 2 x 6 (50 x 150 mm) lumber. It will comfortably seat 10 people. Wide seats positioned both in terms of height and distance from the tabletop ensures easy access and maximum comfort.

Dimensions:
- Length: 10 feet (3 m)
- Width: 67" (1700 mm)
- Height: 29⅞" (758 mm)
- Tabletop width: 34¼" (870 mm)

Card 163

Picnic Table Project
• *10 feet (3 meters) long*
• *Using 2 x 6 (50 x 150 mm) lumber*

Table of Contents - 1

Description	Card 162
Part identification	Card 165
Plans: Imperial measurements	Card 166
Plans: Metric measurements	Card 167
About the measurements	Card 168
Shopping list: Lumber	Card 169
Shopping list: Fixings	Card 170
Cutting list	Card 172
Cut the components to length	Card 174
Cutting plan	Card 175

Card 164

Picnic Table Project
• *10 feet (3 meters) long*
• *Using 2 x 6 (50 x 150 mm) lumber*

Table of Contents - 2

Cut the angled pieces	Card 176
Arrange the legs	Card 178
Assemble the frames	Card 179
Stand the frames	Card 181
Put on the outer boards	Card 183
Check for square and parallel	Card 185
Add the intermediate boards	Card 187
Attach the cleats	Card 189
Add bracing	Card 190
Drill and bolt	Card 191

Picnic Table Project
Card 165
- 10 feet (3 meters) long
- Using 2 x 6 (50 x 150 mm) lumber

Part Identification
- [a] Leg
- [b] Middle rail
- [c] Top rail
- [d] Tabletop board
- [e] Seat board
- [f] Seat cleat
- [g] Table cleat
- [h] Brace

Picnic Table Project
Card 166
- 10 feet (3 meters) long
- Using 2 x 6 (50 x 150 mm) lumber

Plans: Imperial measurements

Picnic Table Project
Card 167
- 10 feet (3 meters) long
- Using 2 x 6 (50 x 150 mm) lumber

Plans: Metric measurements

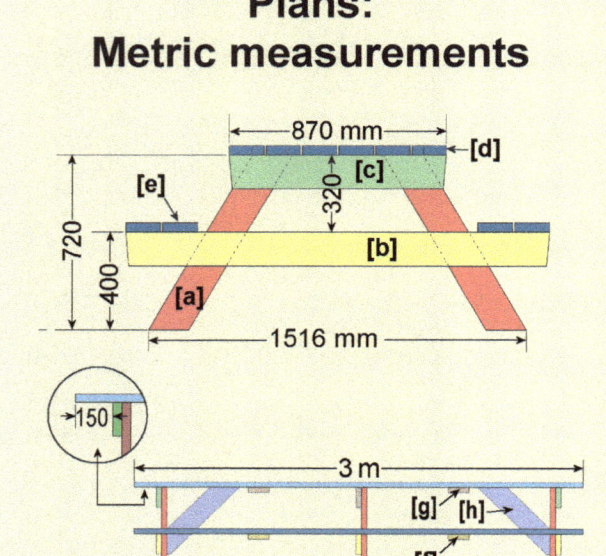

Picnic Table Project
Card 168
- 10 feet (3 meters) long
- Using 2 x 6 (50 x 150 mm) lumber

About the measurements

Length measurements in this project are given in both imperial units (inches) and metric units (millimeters).

When the measurements are presented side by side, the inch measurements are given first followed by the metric equivalent in brackets.

For example: 15-3/4" (400 mm).

Picnic Table Project
- 10 feet (3 meters) long
- Using 2 x 6 (50 x 150 mm) lumber

Card 169

Shopping list: Lumber

Wood size	Length	Qty
2 x 6 (50 x 150 mm)	10 ft (3 m)	17

The lengths provided above are standard stock sizes.

From those lengths you will be able to cut all the pieces that are required to construct the picnic table.

Card 175 shows how you can cut all the pieces from the above lengths to minimize waste.

Picnic Table Project
- 10 feet (3 meters) long
- Using 2 x 6 (50 x 150 mm) lumber

Card 170

Shopping list: Fixings

Exterior wood screws:
- 98 screws 3" (75 mm) long.
- 60 screws 3½" (90 mm) long.

1/2" (12 mm) galvanized coach/carriage bolts:
- 12 bolts 4" (100 mm) long.
- 12 each nuts and washers to match.

Note: Use the 3" (75 mm) screws for the frames, cleats, and braces.
Use the 3½" (90 mm) screws for the seat boards and the tabletop boards.

Picnic Table Project
- 10 feet (3 meters) long
- Using 2 x 6 (50 x 150 mm) lumber

Card 171

Dressed lumber

Dressed lumber is wood that has been planed and smoothed, which makes it smaller than the nominal sizes given.

For example, 2 x 6 (50 x 150 mm) dressed lumber will be 1½" x 5½" (38 x 140 mm) in actual size.

Note: The difference in size will not impact the build, as it is the lengths of the pieces that are important, not so much the size (width and thickness) of the wood.

Picnic Table Project
- 10 feet (3 meters) long
- Using 2 x 6 (50 x 150 mm) lumber

Card 172

Cutting list

2 x 6 (50 x 150 mm) lumber		
Piece ID	Length	Qty
[a] Leg	36" (912 mm)	6
[b] Middle rail	67" (1700 mm)	3
[c] Top rail	34¼" (870 mm)	3
[d] Tabletop board	10 feet (3 m)	6
[e] Seat board	10 feet (3 m)	4
[f] Seat cleat	11¼" (285 mm)	4
[g] Table cleat	34¼" (870 mm)	2
[h] Brace	28⅞" (734 mm)	2

Picnic Table Project
Card 173
- 10 feet (3 meters) long
- Using 2 x 6 (50 x 150 mm) lumber

INSTRUCTIONS

Let's Go!

Start the build

Just follow the cards

Picnic Table Project
Card 174
- 10 feet (3 meters) long
- Using 2 x 6 (50 x 150 mm) lumber

Cut all the pieces

All lumber is 2 x 6 (50 x 150 mm) stock.

Cut all the pieces to the lengths given in the 'Cutting list' (**Card 172**).

All the pieces can be cut from the standard stock lengths that are listed in the 'Shopping list' (**Card 169**).

Following on the next card is a plan drawing showing how all the pieces can be cut from the standard lengths of lumber given in the 'Shopping list'.

Picnic Table Project
Card 175
- 10 feet (3 meters) long
- Using 2 x 6 (50 x 150 mm) lumber

Cutting plan

The drawing below illustrates how all the necessary pieces can be cut from seventeen lengths of 2 x 6 (50 x 150 mm) lumber, each measuring 10 feet (3 m) in length.

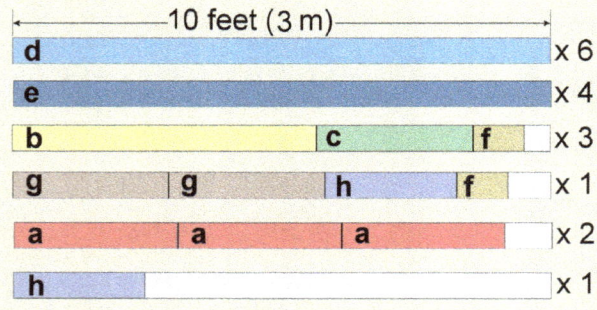

Picnic Table Project
Card 176
- 10 feet (3 meters) long
- Using 2 x 6 (50 x 150 mm) lumber

Cut the angles pieces

Once all the pieces are cut to length, pieces **[a]**, **[b]**, **[c]**, and **[h]** need to have the ends cut at an angle.

Cut the angles according to the drawings below.

- **[a]** cut 6 pieces — 32-3/4" (832 mm) — 30° angle both ends
- **[h]** cut 2 pieces — 28-7/8" (734 mm) — 45° angle both ends
- **[c]** cut 3 pieces — 34-1/4" (870 mm) — 36" (912 mm)
- **[b]** cut 3 pieces — 67" (1700 mm) — 5° angle both ends

Picnic Table Project
- *10 feet (3 meters) long*
- *Using 2 x 6 (50 x 150 mm) lumber*

Card 177

Ready to assemble

At this stage, you should have all the pieces cut as shown below, ready for assembly.

[a]	Leg	6 pieces
[b]	Middle rail	3 pieces
[c]	Top rail	3 pieces
[d]	Tabletop board	6 pieces
[e]	Seat board	4 pieces
[f]	Seat cleat	4 pieces
[g]	Table cleat	2 piece
[h]	Brace	2 pieces

Picnic Table Project
- *10 feet (3 meters) long*
- *Using 2 x 6 (50 x 150 mm) lumber*

Card 178

Arrange the legs

Lay each pair of legs flat on an even surface, spaced according to the plan drawing below. Use a straight-edge to ensure the bottom of both legs are in-line.

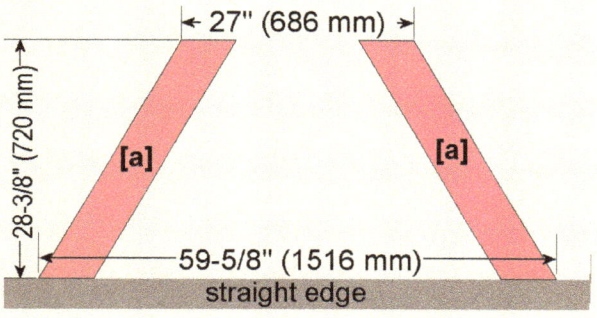

Picnic Table Project
- *10 feet (3 meters) long*
- *Using 2 x 6 (50 x 150 mm) lumber*

Card 179

Assemble the frames

Place cross rails [b] and [c] on legs [a] according to the plan drawing below.
Use four 3" (75 mm) screws at each joint, as illustrated in the drawing below. Do not place screws in the middle of a joint, as that space is reserved for a bolt.

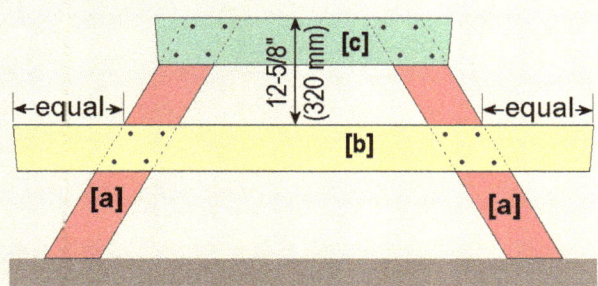

Picnic Table Project
- *10 feet (3 meters) long*
- *Using 2 x 6 (50 x 150 mm) lumber*

Card 180

Screwing

Whenever you're fastening two pieces of wood together with screws, it's important to predrill a **clearance hole** through the top piece.

A **clearance hole** should have the same diameter or slightly larger (but never smaller) than the outside diameter of the screw threads. This allows the screw to go through the top piece smoothly, with the threads only gripping into the bottom piece, ensuring a tight connection between the two parts.

Picnic Table Project — Card 181
- *10 feet (3 meters) long*
- *Using 2 x 6 (50 x 150 mm) lumber*

Stand the frames

Clamp a block flush to the bottom of each leg, as illustrated in the drawing below. This allows the frames to stand independently. You can position the frames and place the boards without needing help from another person.

Picnic Table Project — Card 182
- *10 feet (3 meters) long*
- *Using 2 x 6 (50 x 150 mm) lumber*

Arrange the frames

Now, evenly space the frames approximately so that when the tabletop and seat boards are positioned, they will overhang the frames at each end by 6" (150 mm).

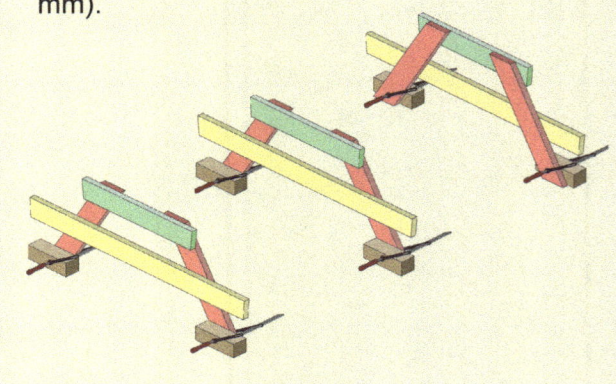

Picnic Table Project — Card 183
- *10 feet (3 meters) long*
- *Using 2 x 6 (50 x 150 mm) lumber*

Put on the outer boards

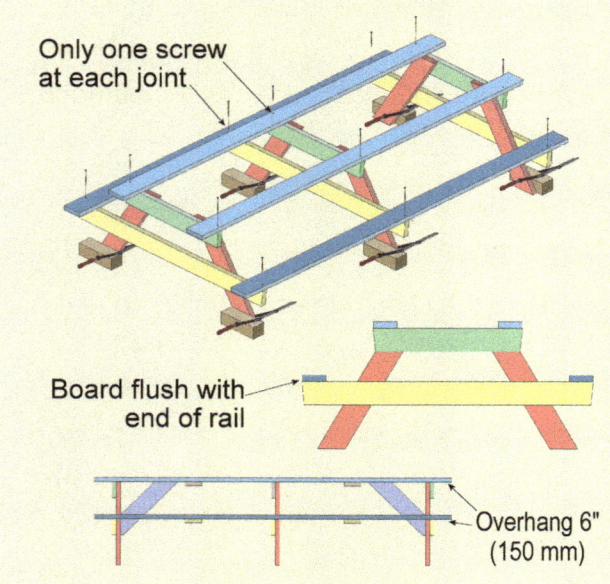

Only one screw at each joint

Board flush with end of rail

Overhang 6" (150 mm)

Picnic Table Project — Card 184
- *10 feet (3 meters) long*
- *Using 2 x 6 (50 x 150 mm) lumber*

Put on the outer boards [explanation]

First, place the outer tabletop and seat boards onto the frame rails, having them overhang each end by 6" (150 mm). Refer to the drawing on the previous card for placement. Secure the boards with **only one screw** at each joint - for the time being. A second screw will be added when the frames have been checked square and parallel.

Use 3½" (90 mm) screws positioned ¾" (19 mm) in from the outside edge of the board.

Picnic Table Project
- 10 feet (3 meters) long
- Using 2 x 6 (50 x 150 mm) lumber

Card 185

Is it square and parallel?

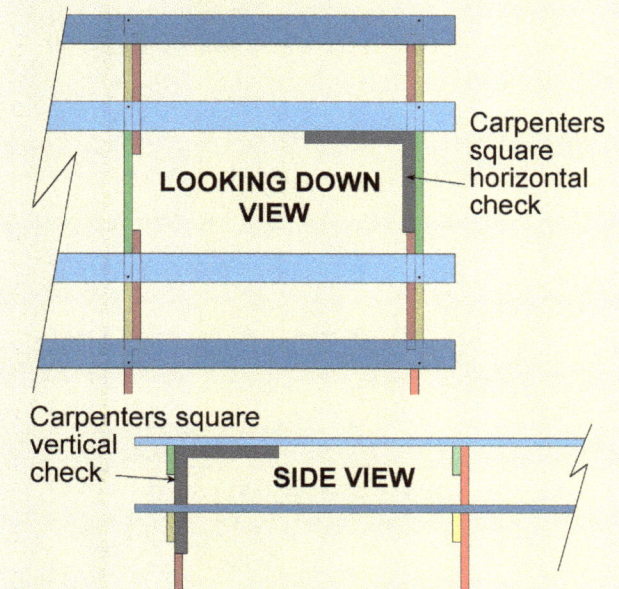

Carpenters square horizontal check

LOOKING DOWN VIEW

Carpenters square vertical check

SIDE VIEW

Picnic Table Project
- 10 feet (3 meters) long
- Using 2 x 6 (50 x 150 mm) lumber

Card 186

Is it square and parallel? [explanation]

Check that the frames are parallel and using a carpenter's square, ensure the frames are square to the tabletop and seat boards, both horizontally and vertically. If necessary, make any straightening adjustments. Then, add a second screw to each joint. This will hold the unit square while you continue to add the intermediate boards.

Picnic Table Project
- 10 feet (3 meters) long
- Using 2 x 6 (50 x 150 mm) lumber

Card 187

Add the intermediate boards

Place the intermediate boards. Ensure the ends are flush and the gaps between the boards are even.

Draw a 'screw line' across both the table and the seats to keep the screws in a straight line.

Picnic Table Project
- 10 feet (3 meters) long
- Using 2 x 6 (50 x 150 mm) lumber

Card 188

Screwing detail

Use 3½" (90 mm) exterior wood screws. Ensure the screws are in a straight line.

Drill clearance holes through the boards prior to screwing.

Picnic Table Project
- *10 feet (3 meters) long*
- *Using 2 x 6 (50 x 150 mm) lumber*

Card 189

Attach the cleats

With the table upside-down, screw cleats across the seats and the tabletop, centered between the frames. Use two 3" (75 mm) screws positioned diagonally across each joint.

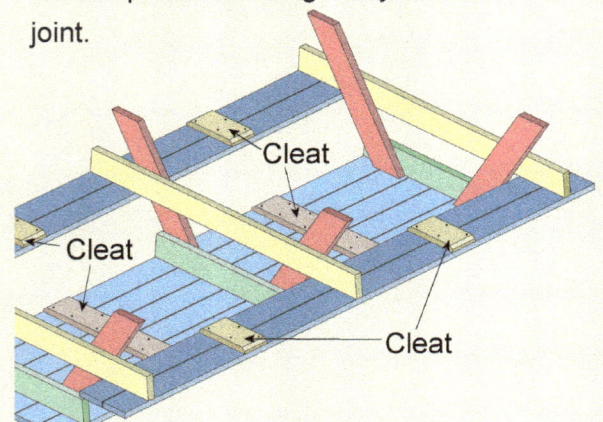

Picnic Table Project
- *10 feet (3 meters) long*
- *Using 2 x 6 (50 x 150 mm) lumber*

Card 190

Add bracing

Ensure the end-frames are square (upright) to the tabletop, and then position each brace as shown in the image below. Screw one end of the brace to the middle rail with two 3" (75 mm) screws, and the other end with 3 screws angled into the tabletop.

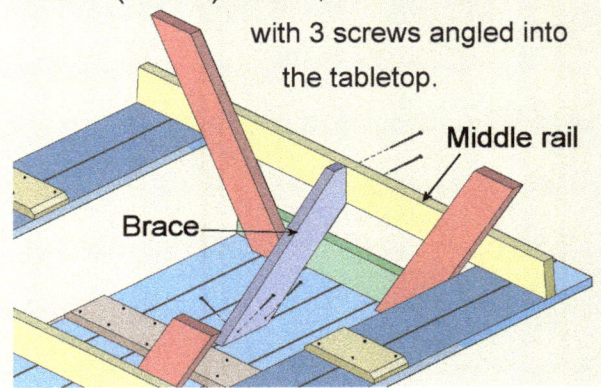

Picnic Table Project
- *10 feet (3 meters) long*
- *Using 2 x 6 (50 x 150 mm) lumber*

Card 191

Drill and bolt

Drill a bolt hole through the center of every leg and rail joint - twelve altogether. Insert 1/2" (12 mm) galvanised bolts, add washers and nuts, and tighten up.

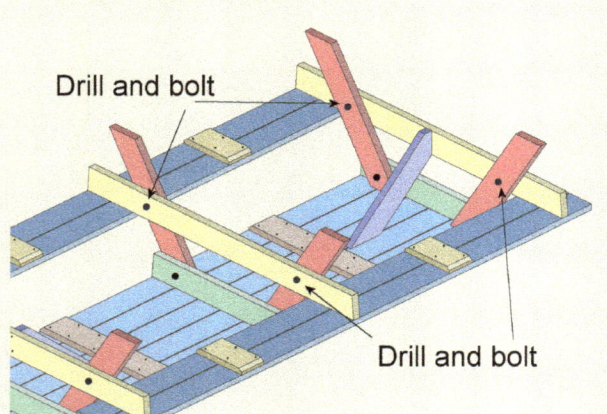

Picnic Table Project
- *10 feet (3 meters) long*
- *Using 2 x 6 (50 x 150 mm) lumber*

Card 192

All finished!

And there it is.
A nice solid, comfortable picnic table that will seat ten people.

Enjoy!

You are now leaving the

10 feet (3 meters) long picnic table project

constructed out of

2 x 6 (50 x 150 mm) lumber

Next up

12 feet (3.6 meters) long picnic table project

using

2 x 4 (50 x 100 mm) lumber

Build your own Picnic Table

12 feet (3.6 meters) long

Using 2 x 4 (50 x 100 mm) lumber

It will comfortably seat 12 people

Just follow the cards →

Card 193

Build Your Own Picnic Table

* *12 feet (3.6 meters) long*
* *Using 2 x 4 (50 x 100 mm) lumber*

Just follow the cards

Card 194

Picnic Table Project
- *12 feet (3.6 meters) long*
- *Using 2 x 4 (50 x 100 mm) lumber*

Description

This picnic table is constructed out of 2 x 4 (50 x 100 mm) lumber. It will comfortably seat 12 people. Wide seats positioned both in terms of height and distance from the tabletop ensures easy access and maximum comfort.

Dimensions:
- Length: 12 feet (3.6 m)
- Width: 67" (1700 mm)
- Height: 29⅞" (758 mm)
- Tabletop width: 34¼" (870 mm)

Card 195

Picnic Table Project
- *12 feet (3.6 meters) long*
- *Using 2 x 4 (50 x 100 mm) lumber*

Table of Contents - 1

Description	Card 194
Part identification	Card 197
Plans: Imperial measurements	Card 198
Plans: Metric measurements	Card 199
About the measurements	Card 200
Shopping list: Lumber	Card 201
Shopping list: Fixings	Card 202
Cutting list	Card 204
Cut the components to length	Card 206
Cutting plan	Card 207

Card 196

Picnic Table Project
- *12 feet (3.6 meters) long*
- *Using 2 x 4 (50 x 100 mm) lumber*

Table of Contents - 2

Cut the angled pieces	Card 208
Arrange the legs	Card 210
Assemble the frames	Card 211
Stand the frames	Card 213
Put on the outer boards	Card 215
Check for square and parallel	Card 217
Add the intermediate boards	Card 219
Attach the cleats	Card 221
Add bracing	Card 222
Drill and bolt	Card 223

Picnic Table Project
Card 197
- *12 feet (3.6 meters) long*
- *Using 2 x 4 (50 x 100 mm) lumber*

Part identification
- [a] Leg
- [b] Middle rail
- [c] Top rail
- [d] Tabletop board
- [e] Seat board
- [f] Seat cleat
- [g] Table cleat
- [h] Brace

Picnic Table Project
Card 198
- *12 feet (3.6 meters) long*
- *Using 2 x 4 (50 x 100 mm) lumber*

Plans: Imperial measurements

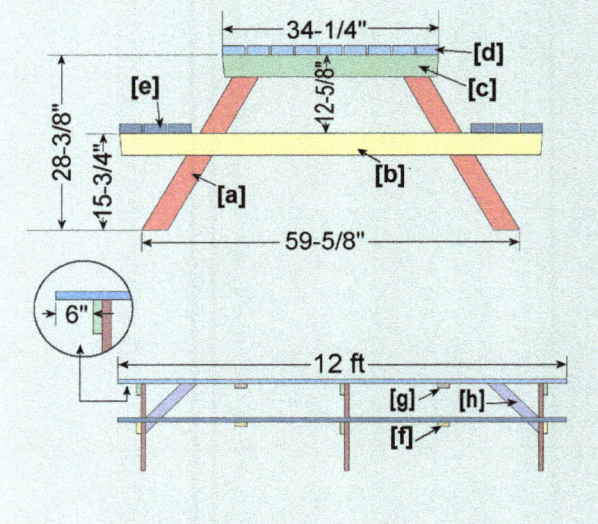

Picnic Table Project
Card 199
- *12 feet (3.6 meters) long*
- *Using 2 x 4 (50 x 100 mm) lumber*

Plans: Metric measurements

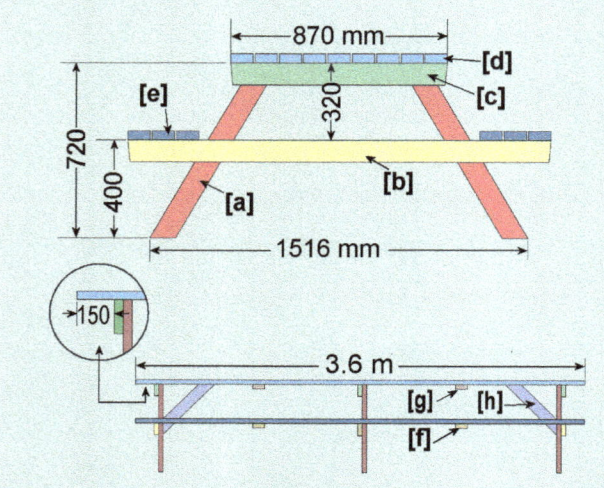

Picnic Table Project
Card 200
- *12 feet (3.6 meters) long*
- *Using 2 x 4 (50 x 100 mm) lumber*

About the measurements

Length measurements in this project are given in both imperial units (inches) and metric units (millimeters).

When the measurements are presented side by side, the inch measurements are given first followed by the metric equivalent in brackets.

For example: 15-3/4" (400 mm).

Card 201

Picnic Table Project
- *12 feet (3.6 meters) long*
- *Using 2 x 4 (50 x 100 mm) lumber*

Shopping list: Lumber

Wood size	Length	Qty
2 x 4 (50 x 100 mm)	12 ft (3.6 m)	20

The lengths provided above are standard stock sizes.

From those lengths you will be able to cut all the pieces that are required to construct the picnic table.

Card 207 shows how you can cut all the pieces from the above lengths to minimize waste.

Card 202

Picnic Table Project
- *12 feet (3.6 meters) long*
- *Using 2 x 4 (50 x 100 mm) lumber*

Shopping list: Fixings

Exterior wood screws:
- 118 screws 3" (75 mm) long.
- 90 screws 3½" (90 mm) long.

1/2" (12 mm) galvanized coach/carriage bolts:
- 12 bolts 4" (100 mm) long.
- 12 each nuts and washers to match.

Note: Use the 3" (75 mm) screws for the frames, cleats, and braces.
Use the 3½" (90 mm) screws for the seat boards and the tabletop boards.

Card 203

Picnic Table Project
- *12 feet (3.6 meters) long*
- *Using 2 x 4 (50 x 100 mm) lumber*

Dressed lumber

Dressed lumber is wood that has been planed and smoothed, which makes it smaller than the nominal sizes given.

For example, 2 x 4 (50 x 100 mm) dressed lumber will be 1½" x 3½" (38 x 89 mm) in actual size.

Note: The difference in size will not impact the build, as it is the lengths of the pieces that are important, not so much the size (width and thickness) of the wood.

Card 204

Picnic Table Project
- *12 feet (3.6 meters) long*
- *Using 2 x 4 (50 x 100 mm) lumber*

Cutting list

2 x 4 (50 x 100 mm) lumber		
Piece ID	Length	Qty
[a] Leg	34¾" (883 mm)	6
[b] Middle rail	67" (1700 mm)	3
[c] Top rail	34¼" (870 mm)	3
[d] Tabletop board	12 feet (3.6 m)	9
[e] Seat board	12 feet (3.6 m)	6
[f] Seat cleat	11¼" (285 mm)	4
[g] Table cleat	34¼" (870 mm)	2
[h] Brace	25" (635 mm)	2

Picnic Table Project
- *12 feet (3.6 meters) long*
- *Using 2 x 4 (50 x 100 mm) lumber*

Card 205

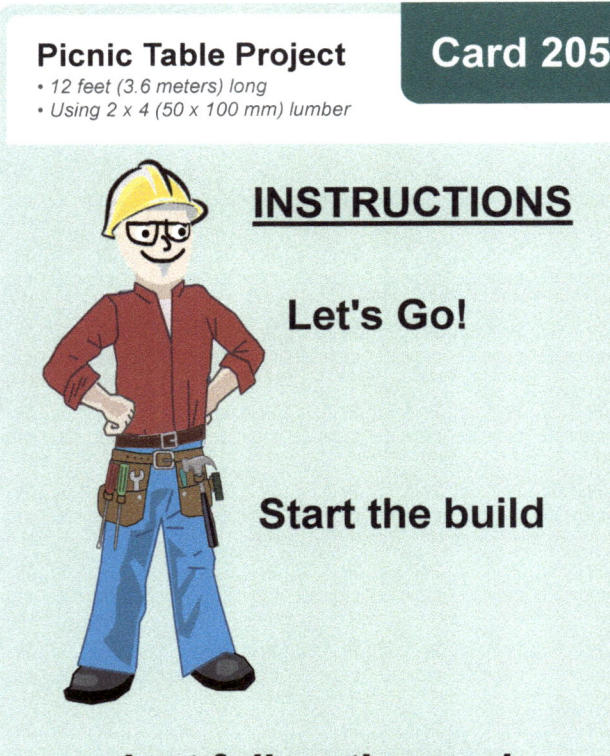

INSTRUCTIONS

Let's Go!

Start the build

Just follow the cards

Picnic Table Project
- *12 feet (3.6 meters) long*
- *Using 2 x 4 (50 x 100 mm) lumber*

Card 206

Cut all the pieces

All lumber is 2 x 4 (50 x 100 mm) stock.

Cut all the pieces to the lengths given in the 'Cutting List' (**Card 204**).

All the pieces can be cut from the standard stock lengths that are listed in the 'Shopping list' (**Card 201**).

Following on the next card is a plan drawing showing how all the pieces can be cut from the standard lengths of lumber given in the 'Shopping list'.

Picnic Table Project
- *12 feet (3.6 meters) long*
- *Using 2 x 4 (50 x 100 mm) lumber*

Card 207

Cutting plan

The drawing below demonstrates how to cut all the necessary components from twenty 2 x 4 (50 x 100 mm) lumber pieces, each measuring 12 ft (3.6m) in length.

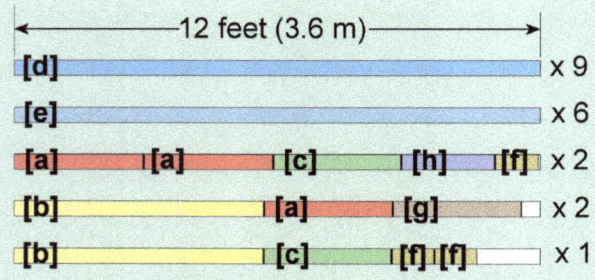

Picnic Table Project
- *12 feet (3.6 meters) long*
- *Using 2 x 4 (50 x 100 mm) lumber*

Card 208

Cut the angles pieces

Once all the pieces are cut to length, pieces **[a]**, **[b]**, **[c]**, and **[h]** need to have the ends cut at an angle. Cut the angles according to the drawings below.

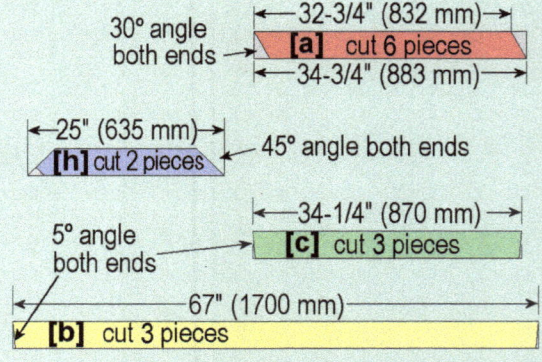

Picnic Table Project
- 12 feet (3.6 meters) long
- Using 2 x 4 (50 x 100 mm) lumber

Card 209

Ready to assemble

At this stage, you should have all the pieces cut as shown below, ready for assembly.

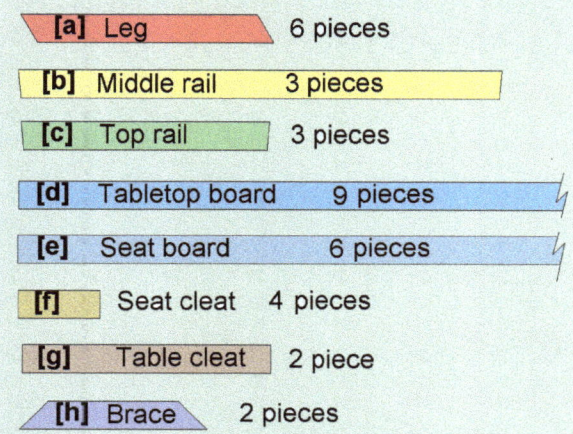

- [a] Leg — 6 pieces
- [b] Middle rail — 3 pieces
- [c] Top rail — 3 pieces
- [d] Tabletop board — 9 pieces
- [e] Seat board — 6 pieces
- [f] Seat cleat — 4 pieces
- [g] Table cleat — 2 piece
- [h] Brace — 2 pieces

Picnic Table Project
- 12 feet (3.6 meters) long
- Using 2 x 4 (50 x 100 mm) lumber

Card 210

Arrange the legs

Lay each pair of legs flat on an even surface, spaced according to the plan drawing below. Use a straight-edge to ensure the bottom of both legs are in-line.

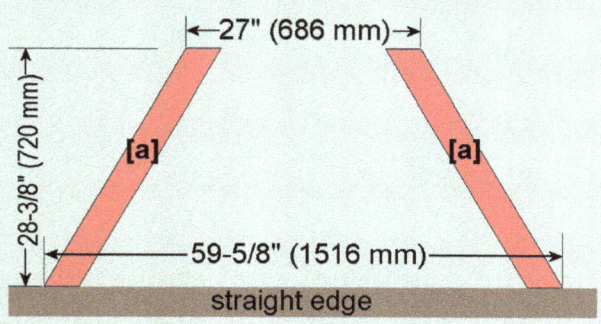

27" (686 mm)
28-3/8" (720 mm)
59-5/8" (1516 mm)
straight edge

Picnic Table Project
- 12 feet (3.6 meters) long
- Using 2 x 4 (50 x 100 mm) lumber

Card 211

Assemble the frames

Place cross rails **[b]** and **[c]** on legs **[a]** according to the plan drawing below.
Use four 3" (75 mm) screws at each joint, as illustrated in the drawing below. Do not place screws in the middle of a joint, as that space is reserved for a bolt.

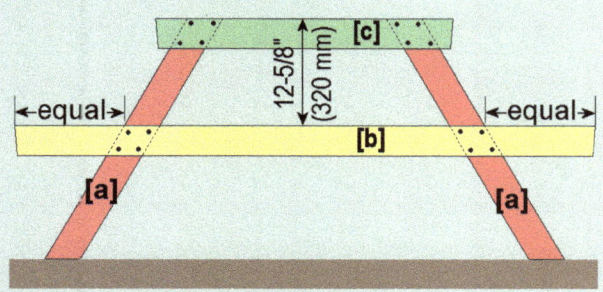

12-5/8" (320 mm)

Picnic Table Project
- 12 feet (3.6 meters) long
- Using 2 x 4 (50 x 100 mm) lumber

Card 212

 ### Screwing

Whenever you're fastening two pieces of wood together with screws, it's important to predrill a **clearance hole** through the top piece.

A **clearance hole** should have the same diameter or slightly larger (but never smaller) than the outside diameter of the screw threads. This allows the screw to go through the top piece smoothly, with the threads only gripping into the bottom piece, ensuring a tight connection between the two parts.

Picnic Table Project — Card 213
- *12 feet (3.6 meters) long*
- *Using 2 x 4 (50 x 100 mm) lumber*

Stand the frames

Clamp a block flush to the bottom of each leg, as illustrated in the drawing below. This allows the frames to stand independently. You can position the frames and place the boards without needing help from another person.

Picnic Table Project — Card 214
- *12 feet (3.6 meters) long*
- *Using 2 x 4 (50 x 100 mm) lumber*

Arrange the frames

Evenly space the frames approximately so that when the tabletop and seat boards are positioned, they will overhang the frames at each end by 6" (150 mm).

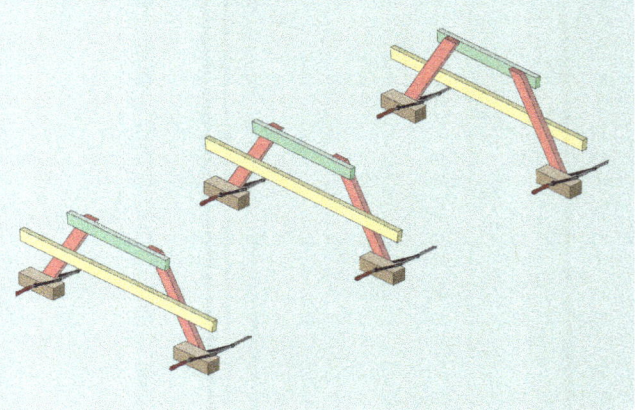

Picnic Table Project — Card 215
- *12 feet (3.6 meters) long*
- *Using 2 x 4 (50 x 100 mm) lumber*

Put on the outer boards

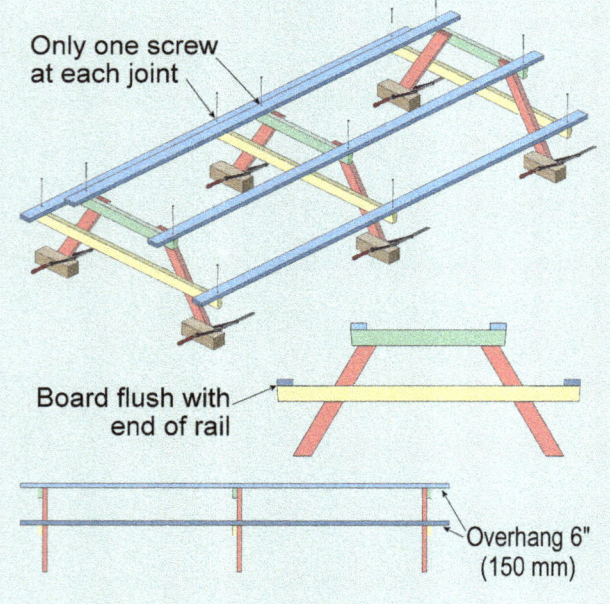

Only one screw at each joint

Board flush with end of rail

Overhang 6" (150 mm)

Picnic Table Project — Card 216
- *12 feet (3.6 meters) long*
- *Using 2 x 4 (50 x 100 mm) lumber*

Put on the outer boards [explanation]

First, place the outer tabletop and seat boards onto the frame rails, having them overhang each end by 6" (150 mm). Refer to the drawing on the previous card for placement.

Secure the boards with **only one screw** at each joint - for the time being. A second screw will be added when the frames have been checked square and parallel.

Use 3½" (90 mm) screws positioned ⅝" (15 mm) in from the outside edge of the board.

Picnic Table Project
- *12 feet (3.6 meters) long*
- *Using 2 x 4 (50 x 100 mm) lumber*

Card 217

Is it square and parallel?

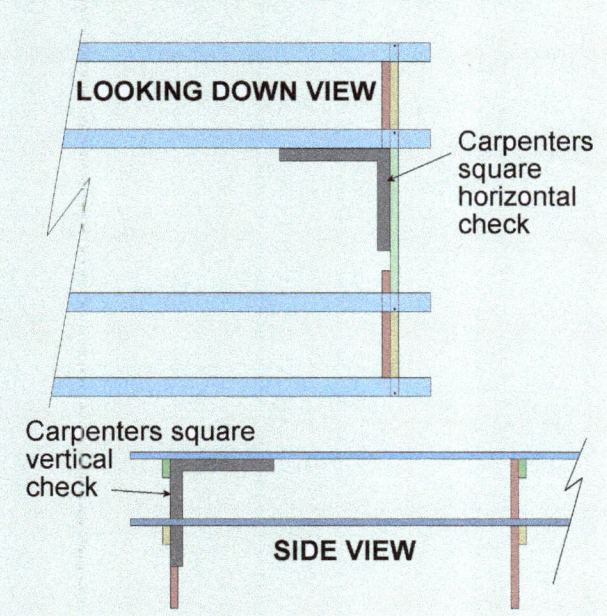

Picnic Table Project
- *12 feet (3.6 meters) long*
- *Using 2 x 4 (50 x 100 mm) lumber*

Card 218

Is it square and parallel? [explanation]

Check that the frames are parallel and using a carpenter's square, ensure the frames are square to the tabletop and seat boards, both horizontally and vertically. If necessary, make any straightening adjustments. Then, add a second screw to each joint. This will hold the unit square while you continue to add the intermediate boards.

Picnic Table Project
- *12 feet (3.6 meters) long*
- *Using 2 x 4 (50 x 100 mm) lumber*

Card 219

Add the intermediate boards

Place the intermediate boards. Ensure the ends are flush and the gaps between the boards are even. Draw a 'screw line' across both the table and the seats to keep the screws in a straight line.

Picnic Table Project
- *12 feet (3.6 meters) long*
- *Using 2 x 4 (50 x 100 mm) lumber*

Card 220

Screwing detail

Use 3½" (90 mm) exterior wood screws. Ensure the screws are in a straight line.

Drill clearance holes through the boards prior to screwing.

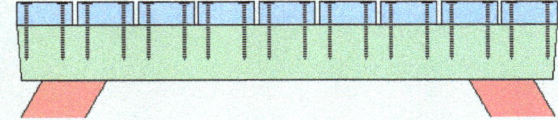

Picnic Table Project
Card 221
- *12 feet (3.6 meters) long*
- *Using 2 x 4 (50 x 100 mm) lumber*

Attach the cleats

With the table upside-down, screw cleats across the seats and the tabletop, centered between the frames. Use two 3" (75 mm) screws positioned diagonally across each joint.

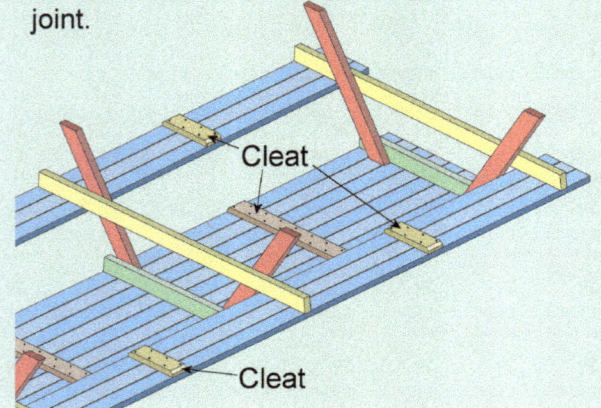

Picnic Table Project
Card 222
- *12 feet (3.6 meters) long*
- *Using 2 x 4 (50 x 100 mm) lumber*

Add bracing

Ensure the end-frames are square (upright) to the tabletop, and then position each brace as shown in the image below. Screw one end of the brace to the middle rail with two 3" (75 mm) screws, and the other end with 3 screws angled into the tabletop.

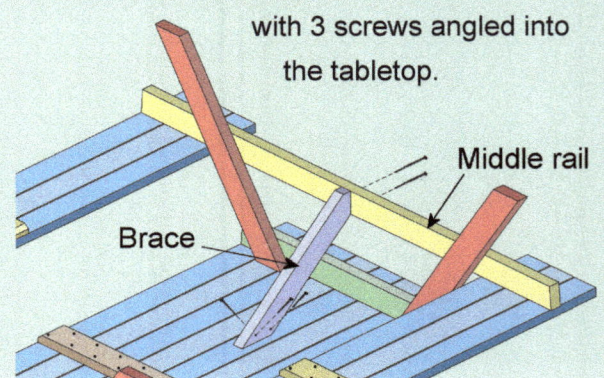

Picnic Table Project
Card 223
- *12 feet (3.6 meters) long*
- *Using 2 x 4 (50 x 100 mm) lumber*

Drill and bolt

Drill a bolt hole through the center of every leg and rail joint - twelve altogether.
Insert 1/2" (12 mm) galvanised bolts, add washers and nuts, and tighten them up.

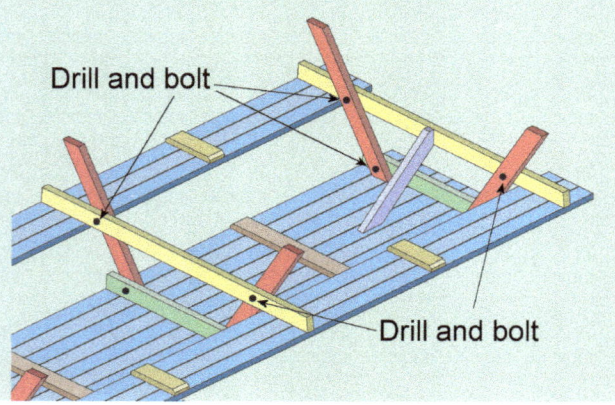

Picnic Table Project
Card 224
- *12 feet (3.6 meters) long*
- *Using 2 x 4 (50 x 100 mm) lumber*

All finished!

And there it is.
A nice solid, comfortable picnic table that will seat twelve people.

Enjoy!

You are now leaving the

12 feet (3.6 meters) long picnic table project

constructed out of

2 x 4 (50 x 100 mm) lumber

Next up

12 feet (3.6 meters) long picnic table project

using

2 x 6 (50 x 150 mm) lumber

Build your own Picnic Table

12 feet (3.6 meters) long

Using 2 x 6 (50 x 150 mm) lumber

It will comfortably seat 12 people

Just follow the cards →

Card 225

Build Your Own Picnic Table

* *12 feet (3.6 meters) long*
* *Using 2 x 6 (50 x 150 mm) lumber*

Just follow the cards

Card 226

Picnic Table Project
* *12 feet (3.6 meters) long*
* *Using 2 x 6 (50 x 150 mm) lumber*

Description

This picnic table is constructed out of 2 x 6 (50 x 150 mm) lumber. It will comfortably seat 12 people. Wide seats positioned both in terms of height and distance from the tabletop ensures easy access and maximum comfort.

Dimensions:
- Length: 12 feet (3.6 m)
- Width: 67" (1700 mm)
- Height: 29⅞" (758 mm)
- Tabletop width: 34¼" (870 mm)

Card 227

Picnic Table Project
* *12 feet (3.6 meters) long*
* *Using 2 x 6 (50 x 150 mm) lumber*

Table of Contents - 1

Description	Card 226
Part identification	Card 229
Plans: Imperial measurements	Card 230
Plans: Metric measurements	Card 231
About the measurements	Card 232
Shopping list: Lumber	Card 233
Shopping list: Fixings	Card 234
Cutting list	Card 236
Cut the components to length	Card 238
Cutting plan	Card 239

Card 228

Picnic Table Project
* *12 feet (3.6 meters) long*
* *Using 2 x 6 (50 x 150 mm) lumber*

Table of Contents - 2

Cut the angled pieces	Card 240
Arrange the legs	Card 242
Assemble the frames	Card 243
Stand the frames	Card 245
Put on the outer boards	Card 247
Check for square and parallel	Card 249
Add the intermediate boards	Card 251
Attach the cleats	Card 253
Add bracing	Card 254
Drill and bolt	Card 255

Picnic Table Project
Card 229
- *12 feet (3.6 meters) long*
- *Using 2 x 6 (50 x 150 mm) lumber*

Part Identification
- [a] Leg
- [b] Middle rail
- [c] Top rail
- [d] Tabletop board
- [e] Seat board
- [f] Seat cleat
- [g] Table cleat
- [h] Brace

Picnic Table Project
Card 230
- *12 feet (3.6 meters) long*
- *Using 2 x 6 (50 x 150 mm) lumber*

Plans: Imperial measurements

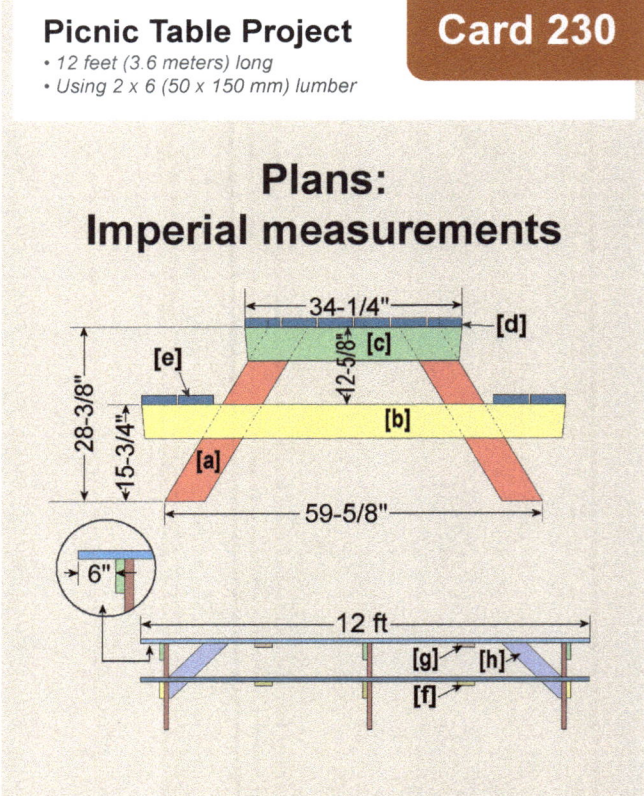

Picnic Table Project
Card 231
- *12 feet (3.6 meters) long*
- *Using 2 x 6 (50 x 150 mm) lumber*

Plans: Metric measurements

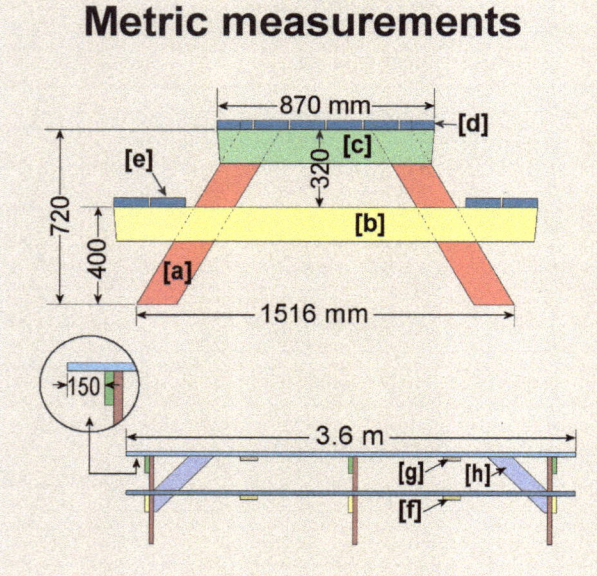

Picnic Table Project
Card 232
- *12 feet (3.6 meters) long*
- *Using 2 x 6 (50 x 150 mm) lumber*

About the measurements

Length measurements in this project are given in both imperial units (inches) and metric units (millimeters).

When the measurements are presented side by side, the inch measurements are given first followed by the metric equivalent in brackets.

For example: 15-3/4" (400 mm).

Card 233

Picnic Table Project
- 12 feet (3.6 meters) long
- Using 2 x 6 (50 x 150 mm) lumber

Shopping list: Lumber

Wood size	Length	Qty
2 x 6 (50 x 150 mm)	12 ft (3.6 m)	15

The lengths provided above are standard stock sizes.

From those lengths you will be able to cut all the pieces that are required to construct the picnic table.

Card 239 shows how you can cut all the pieces from the above lengths to minimize waste.

Card 234

Picnic Table Project
- 12 feet (3.6 meters) long
- Using 2 x 6 (50 x 150 mm) lumber

Shopping list: Fixings

Exterior wood screws:
- 98 screws 3" (75 mm) long.
- 60 screws 3½" (90 mm) long.

1/2" (12 mm) galvanized coach/carriage bolts:
- 12 bolts 4" (100 mm) long.
- 12 each nuts and washers to match.

Note: Use the 3" (75 mm) screws for the frames, cleats, and braces.
Use the 3½" (90 mm) screws for the seat boards and the tabletop boards.

Card 235

Picnic Table Project
- 12 feet (3.6 meters) long
- Using 2 x 6 (50 x 150 mm) lumber

Dressed lumber

Dressed lumber is wood that has been planed and smoothed, which makes it smaller than the nominal sizes given.

For example, 2 x 6 (50 x 150 mm) dressed lumber will be 1½" x 5½" (38 x 140 mm) in actual size.

Note: The difference in size will not impact the build, as it is the lengths of the pieces that are important, not so much the size (width and thickness) of the wood.

Card 236

Picnic Table Project
- 12 feet (3.6 meters) long
- Using 2 x 6 (50 x 150 mm) lumber

Cutting list

2 x 6 (50 x 150 mm) lumber		
Piece ID	Length	Qty
[a] Leg	36" (912 mm)	6
[b] Middle rail	67" (1700 mm)	3
[c] Top rail	34¼" (870 mm)	3
[d] Tabletop board	12 feet (3.6 m)	6
[e] Seat board	12 feet (3.6 m)	4
[f] Seat cleat	11¼" (285 mm)	4
[g] Table cleat	34¼" (870 mm)	2
[h] Brace	28⅞" (734 mm)	2

Picnic Table Project
Card 237
- 12 feet (3.6 meters) long
- Using 2 x 6 (50 x 150 mm) lumber

INSTRUCTIONS

Let's Go!

Start the build

Just follow the cards

Picnic Table Project
Card 238
- 12 feet (3.6 meters) long
- Using 2 x 6 (50 x 150 mm) lumber

Cut all the pieces

All lumber is 2 x 6 (50 x 150 mm) stock.

Cut all the pieces to the lengths given in the 'Cutting list' (**Card 236**).

All the pieces can be cut from the standard stock lengths that are listed in the 'Shopping list' (**Card 233**).

Following on the next card is a plan drawing showing how all the pieces can be cut from the standard lengths of lumber given in the 'Shopping list'.

Picnic Table Project
Card 239
- 12 feet (3.6 meters) long
- Using 2 x 6 (50 x 150 mm) lumber

Cutting plan

The drawing below illustrates how all the necessary pieces can be cut from fifteen lengths of 2 x 6 (50 x 150 mm) lumber, each measuring 12 ft (3.6 m) in length.

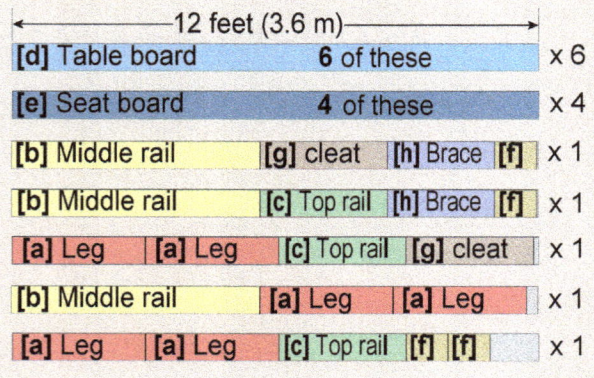

Picnic Table Project
Card 240
- 12 feet (3.6 meters) long
- Using 2 x 6 (50 x 150 mm) lumber

Cut the angles pieces

Once all the pieces are cut to length, pieces **[a]**, **[b]**, **[c]**, and **[h]** need to have the ends cut at an angle. Cut the angles according to the drawings below.

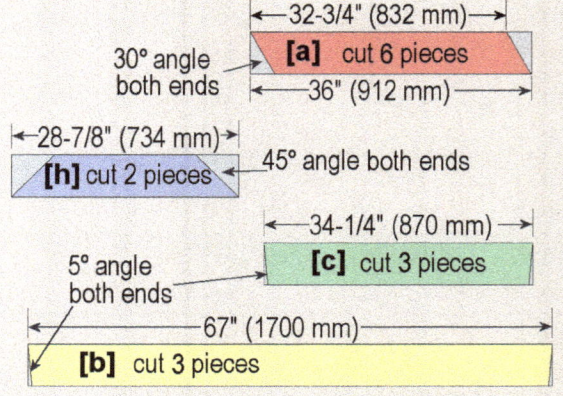

Picnic Table Project
- 12 feet (3.6 meters) long
- Using 2 x 6 (50 x 150 mm) lumber

Card 241

Ready to assemble

At this stage, you should have all the pieces cut as shown below, ready for assembly.

[a]	Leg	6 pieces
[b]	Middle rail	3 pieces
[c]	Top rail	3 pieces
[d]	Tabletop board	6 pieces
[e]	Seat board	4 pieces
[f]	Seat cleat	4 pieces
[g]	Table cleat	2 piece
[h]	Brace	2 pieces

Picnic Table Project
- 12 feet (3.6 meters) long
- Using 2 x 6 (50 x 150 mm) lumber

Card 242

Arrange the legs

Lay each pair of legs flat on an even surface, spaced according to the plan drawing below. Use a straight-edge to ensure the bottom of both legs are in-line.

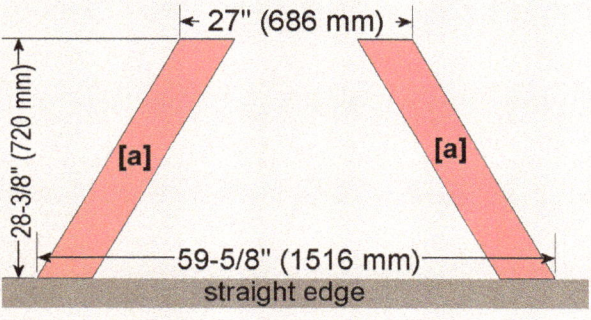

Picnic Table Project
- 12 feet (3.6 meters) long
- Using 2 x 6 (50 x 150 mm) lumber

Card 243

Assemble the frames

Place cross rails [b] and [c] on legs [a] according to the plan drawing below.
Use four 3" (75 mm) screws at each joint, as illustrated in the drawing below. Do not place screws in the middle of a joint, as that space is reserved for a bolt.

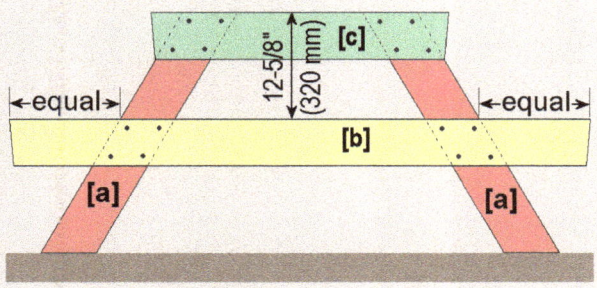

Picnic Table Project
- 12 feet (3.6 meters) long
- Using 2 x 6 (50 x 150 mm) lumber

Card 244

Screwing

Whenever you're fastening two pieces of wood together with screws, it's important to predrill a **clearance hole** through the top piece.

A **clearance hole** should have the same diameter or slightly larger (but never smaller) than the outside diameter of the screw threads. This allows the screw to go through the top piece smoothly, with the threads only gripping into the bottom piece, ensuring a tight connection between the two parts.

Picnic Table Project
- *12 feet (3.6 meters) long*
- *Using 2 x 6 (50 x 150 mm) lumber*

Card 245

Stand the frames

Clamp a block flush to the bottom of each leg, as illustrated in the drawing below. This allows the frames to stand independently. You can position the frames and place the boards without needing help from another person

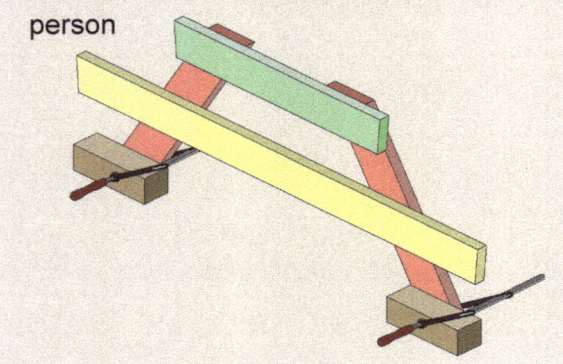

Picnic Table Project
- *12 feet (3.6 meters) long*
- *Using 2 x 6 (50 x 150 mm) lumber*

Card 246

Arrange the frames

Evenly space the frames approximately so that when the tabletop and seat boards are positioned, they will overhang the frames at each end by 6" (150 mm).

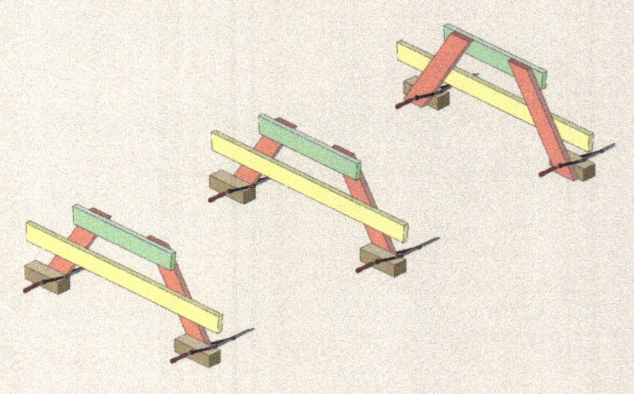

Picnic Table Project
- *12 feet (3.6 meters) long*
- *Using 2 x 6 (50 x 150 mm) lumber*

Card 247

Put on the outer boards

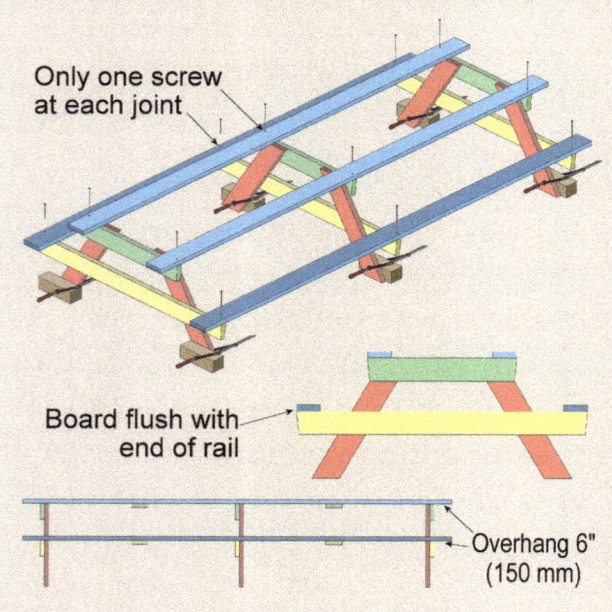

Only one screw at each joint

Board flush with end of rail

Overhang 6" (150 mm)

Picnic Table Project
- *12 feet (3.6 meters) long*
- *Using 2 x 6 (50 x 150 mm) lumber*

Card 248

Put on the outer boards [explanation]

First, place the outer tabletop and seat boards onto the frame rails, having them overhang each end by 6" (150 mm). Refer to the drawing on the previous card for placement.

Secure the boards with <u>**only one screw**</u> at each joint - for the time being. A second screw will be added when the frames have been checked square and parallel.

Use 3½" (90 mm) screws positioned ¾" (19 mm) in from the outside edge of the board.

Picnic Table Project
- *12 feet (3.6 meters) long*
- *Using 2 x 6 (50 x 150 mm) lumber*

Card 249

Is it square and parallel?

LOOKING DOWN VIEW

Carpenters square horizontal check

Carpenters square vertical check

SIDE VIEW

Picnic Table Project
- *12 feet (3.6 meters) long*
- *Using 2 x 6 (50 x 150 mm) lumber*

Card 250

Is it square and parallel? [explanation]

Check that the frames are parallel and using a carpenter's square, ensure the frames are square to the tabletop and seat boards, both horizontally and vertically. If necessary, make any straightening adjustments. Then, add a second screw to each joint. This will hold the unit square while you continue to add the intermediate boards.

Picnic Table Project
- *12 feet (3.6 meters) long*
- *Using 2 x 6 (50 x 150 mm) lumber*

Card 251

Add the intermediate boards

Place the intermediate boards. Ensure the ends are flush and the gaps between the boards are even. Draw a 'screw line' across both the table and the seats to keep the screws in a straight line.

Picnic Table Project
- *12 feet (3.6 meters) long*
- *Using 2 x 6 (50 x 150 mm) lumber*

Card 252

Screwing detail

Use 3½" (90 mm) exterior wood screws. Ensure the screws are in a straight line.

Drill clearance holes through the boards prior to screwing.

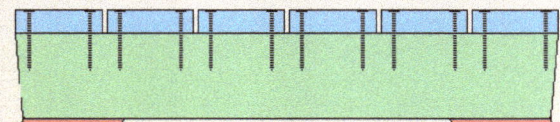

Picnic Table Project
Card 253
- *12 feet (3.6 meters) long*
- *Using 2 x 6 (50 x 150 mm) lumber*

Attach the cleats

With the table upside-down, screw cleats across the seats and the tabletop, centered between the frames. Use two 3" (75 mm) screws positioned diagonally across each joint.

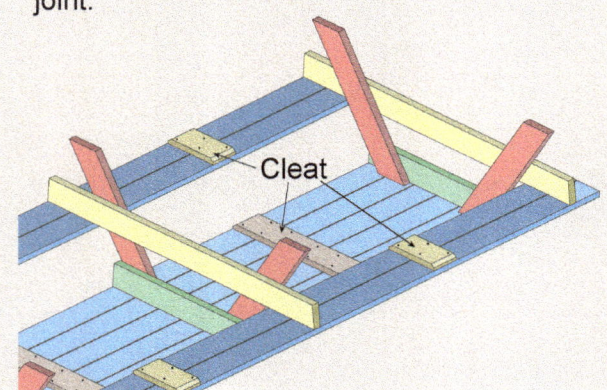
Cleat

Picnic Table Project
Card 254
- *12 feet (3.6 meters) long*
- *Using 2 x 6 (50 x 150 mm) lumber*

Add bracing

Ensure the end-frames are square (upright) to the tabletop, and then position each brace as shown in the image below. Screw one end of the brace to the middle rail with two 2" (75 mm) screws, and the other end with 3 screws angled into the tabletop.

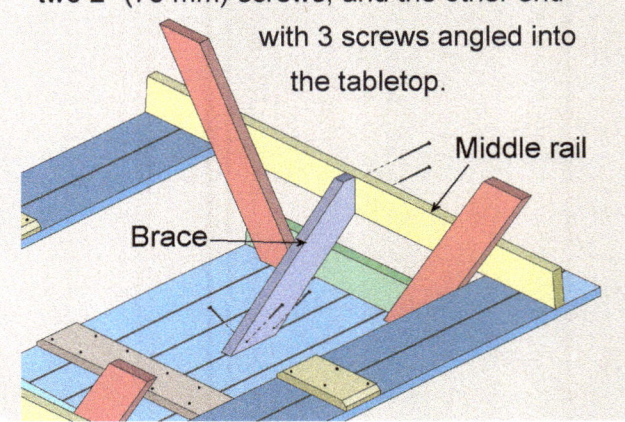
Middle rail
Brace

Picnic Table Project
Card 255
- *12 feet (3.6 meters) long*
- *Using 2 x 6 (50 x 150 mm) lumber*

Drill and bolt

Drill a bolt hole through the center of every leg and rail joint - twelve altogether.
Insert 1/2" (12 mm) galvanised bolts, add washers and nuts, and tighten them up.

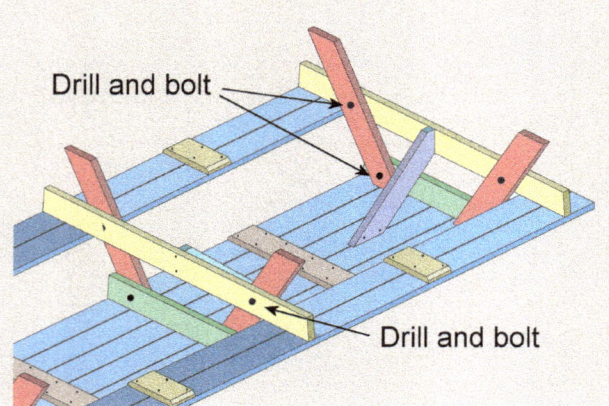
Drill and bolt
Drill and bolt

Picnic Table Project
Card 256
- *12 feet (3.6 meters) long*
- *Using 2 x 6 (50 x 150 mm) lumber*

All finished!

And there it is.
A nice solid, comfortable picnic table that will seat twelve people.

Enjoy!

Picnic Table Project
Helpful Information — Card 257

Table of Contents

The Author	Card 258
Type of wood to use	Card 259
Wood sizes	Card 260
Measurements given	Card 261
Screwing	Card 262
Types of screws to use	Card 263
Disclaimer	Card 264

Picnic Table Project
Helpful Information — Card 258

The Author

Les Kenny has been creating and authoring woodworking projects for many years, with an online presence spanning almost 25 years. Although mostly retired now, he occasionally works on projects and continues to write. Les is a husband, a father of four, and a proud grandfather of seven. You can find his website at leskenny.com.

Picnic Table Project
Helpful Information — Card 259

Type of wood to use

Because picnic tables are mostly used outside, you will need a wood that is suitable for outdoor use. Therefore, consider using a treated lumber such as treated pine or other wood that has a natural resistance to decay, such as cedar or redwood

Use a dressed lumber, which is wood that has been planed or smoothed.

Picnic Table Project
Helpful Information — Card 260

Wood sizes

Use 2 x 4 (50 x 100 mm) or 2 x 6 (50 x 150 mm) dressed lumber for all projects. Dressed lumber is wood that has been planed and smoothed, making it smaller than the nominal sizes given.
• 2 x 4 (50 x 100 mm) dressed lumber will measure 1½" x 3½" (38 x 89 mm) in actual size.
• 2 x 6 (50 x 150 mm) dressed lumber will measure 1½" x 5½" (38 x 140 mm) in actual size.
The difference in size between 'nominal' and 'actual' will not impact the build.

Picnic Table Project
Helpful Information — Card 261

Measurements given

All length measurements throughout this project are provided in both imperial units (feet and/or inches) and metric units (millimeters). When presented side by side, the standard (inch) measurements are given first followed by the metric equivalent in brackets. For example: 15-3/4" (400 mm). Likewise, the size of the wood i.e., the thickness and width is given in similar fashion. For example: 2 x 4 (50 x 100 mm).

Picnic Table Project
Helpful Information — Card 262

Screwing

In all instances, when screwing two pieces of wood together, predrill a clearance hole through the top piece.

A clearance hole is a hole the same diameter or marginally bigger (but not smaller) than the outside diameter of the threads on a screw. This allows the screw to pass all the way through the top piece with the thread only biting into the under piece allowing the two parts to be pulled tight together, avoiding "jacking" and eliminating the chance of the top piece splitting.

Picnic Table Project
Helpful Information — Card 263

Types of screws to use

Use exterior-type screws, such as stainless steel or coated outdoor screws. Flat or countersunk screw heads are recommended to ensure the screw heads sit flush with the surface of the boards. Common choices include #8 and #10 deck screws. The #8 screw has a diameter of 5/32" (4.17 mm), while the #10 screw is slightly larger with a diameter of 3/16" (4.83 mm). For frames, cleats, and braces, use 3" (75 mm) long screws, and for seat boards and tabletop boards, use 3½" (90 mm) long screws.

Picnic Table Project
Helpful Information — Card 264

Disclaimer

While every effort has been made to ensure accuracy, the author, Les Kenny, accepts no responsibility for any incorrect information, omissions, or other irregularities in this book. Users undertake the projects at their own risk.

www.ingramcontent.com/pod-product-compliance
Lightning Source LLC
Chambersburg PA
CBHW042359070526
44585CB00029B/2991